Henry
WADSWORTH
LONGFELLOW
IN PORTLAND

MW00655368

Henry WADSWORTH LONGFELLOW
IN PORTLAND

The Fireside Poet of Maine

JOHN WILLIAM BABIN
and ALLAN M. LEVINSKY

Foreword by Herb Adams

THE
History
PRESS

Published by The History Press
Charleston, SC 29403
www.historypress.net

Copyright © 2015 by John William Babin and Allan Levinsky
All rights reserved

Front cover town image courtesy of the Collections of Maine State Museum and Maine
Historical Society. Longfellow image courtesy of the George J. Mitchell Department of
Special Collections and Archives, Bowdoin College Library, Brunswick, Maine.

First published 2015

Manufactured in the United States

ISBN 978.1.62619.499.1

Library of Congress Control Number: 2015947041

Notice: The information in this book is true and complete to the best of our knowledge. It is
offered without guarantee on the part of the authors or The History Press. The authors and
The History Press disclaim all liability in connection with the use of this book.

All rights reserved. No part of this book may be reproduced or transmitted in any form
whatsoever without prior written permission from the publisher except in the case of brief
quotations embodied in critical articles and reviews.

CONTENTS

FOREWORD

As a teacher and tour guide, one of the best things about the Wadsworth-Longfellow House is that the family has never left it. No, not in the sense that spirits walk the halls—though some say they do. In the sense that this was once a real home, a place of real personalities, of love, loss, tears and joys and a place where a family really lived real life. This aura lingers—in that sense, the Longfellow house is uniquely a home, and a family's blessing still surrounds it.

All houses where people once lived, felt loss, knew joy and passed on "are haunted houses," as wrote Longfellow in his older years. I have no doubt that he was thinking about the home he knew as a boy.

Portland and the Wadsworth-Longfellow House were born together, in 1786. That year, the tiny peninsula seaport separated from old Falmouth town and became infant Portland. Also that same year, cartloads of fresh brick were hauled uphill from local brickyards to the cellar site along the dusty back road out of town, where General Wadsworth was building a new home so far from the center of things that it was considered a folly. But it was different then, and it is different now.

As an old Atlantic seaport, Portland is blessed with several remarkable mansion homes. Visitors can still see the George Tate House in Stroudwater, the home of the king's last royal mast agent and the very last mast agent's house still standing in America. In town, the Victoria Mansion still awes visitors with the no-holds-barred rococo Gilded Age oak, frescoes, stained glass and palatial gilding worthy of its builder, Mainer and hotel magnate

Ruggles Morse. It is the best remaining example of high Victorian living left in America. Tate was an eighteenth-century millionaire and Morse a nineteenth-century multimillionaire. Their houses are meant to awe as symbols of status and grand mansions that still make for memorable visits. Yet one wonders: were there people here? Was this ever a hearth and a home?

Longfellow's boyhood house was exactly that—and it still is. It was once a crowed place and still feels so. Parents, children, in-laws, maiden aunts and visitors filled its three floors. Its sloping floors and favorite spots still feel a bit battered and beloved; well-lived rooms have a sense of smiles and lives worn with tears. Family clutter sits where it should be. It is as if the family is still there, just out of sight in the snug kitchen, happy to be hosts, pleased with visitors. The halls are open now but never really empty. The world that cannot be stopped still rushes by outside, but here the present pauses and takes its hat off at the door.

On the great stone front doorstep, young Zilpah Wadsworth, the poet's future mother, once blushingly presented silk banners to the city militia. In the great parlor inside, once the biggest room in Portland, family members married, balls were danced and Henry's favorite flute still sits atop the family piano. (In the then-distant twentieth century, the infant radio station WCSH broadcast patriotic tunes played on that very piano, probably Maine's first piano to take to the novel airwaves.)

A favorite room for the family, and for visitors still, is the dining room, small and snug, handy by the warm smell of the kitchen. Here, by day, Stephen Longfellow, the poet's father, taught law to young lawyers-to-be; by night, books aside, the family dined around the crowded table in the glow of lamps and love. Even now, in low light, the room feels of family.

And upstairs, in the back bedroom, young Anne Longfellow, the poet's sister, widowed in her youth, once sat by her fireplace wrapped in blankets and wept. By her room, in the plaster wall of the stairs to the third floor, a tiny girl's handprint remains. Her name—Eliza—still exists above it in childish handwriting. She died young; it is all that is left of her.

Her nephew, Henry, passed by it every night of his young life climbing to his boyhood bedroom. As an old man, his shoulders brushed by it every night on visits as he mounted narrow stairs to his favorite adult bedroom above. What did he think about the long-lost aunt he never knew?

Henry Wadsworth Longfellow, by then the most famous man in America, climbed those stairs the last summer of his life while visiting in 1881. By the spring of 1882, he had passed on. It fell to Anne, his younger sister, to hold the memories of the house until the twentieth century, when she left it to us. She changed nothing, and nothing since has changed inside.

Once, from her front windows, you could see Portland Head Light flashing far down the coast. From the back windows, one could hear waves washing against the shores of Back Cove. Now the city has hemmed everything in—including the memories, safely inside. We need a few places like this. America is a very young country, as the world goes, and has a long trail ahead. Homes like this carry the musing visitor forward, as much as back, in thought.

The Freudians may drill Longfellow and come up dry. The poet wrote about an America he loved for a world he believed in, and he spared in his verses none of the personal pain life dealt him (and it dealt him plenty) nor any of the sentimental optimism about mankind that hasty cynics dismiss as all of him. They are wrong.

When Longfellow passed on in 1882, the elderly Ralph Waldo Emerson, sweet but senile, was led up to view his old friend one last time. "That man has a beautiful face," sighed Emerson, "but I have quite forgotten his name."

America has never forgotten Longfellow, and he never forgot the Portland home—a home, in every sense—that framed his life and made his memories warm. The family called the house the "Old Original." Thoughtful workers here are lucky people. Visitors can still find the past, but also the future, if they look quietly enough.

And all, in many ways, will find this one ancient home that is never alone or empty.

–HERB ADAMS
Maine Historian

ACKNOWLEDGEMENTS

To my mom, Gloria Ann Latini Babin: thanks, Mom! I'll never forget the first time you brought me to the Longfellow House when I was but a wee lad. I still have the same feeling today as I did as a child walking up the stairway to the second floor. Some things you never forget! To Sofia Yalouris, image services coordinator for the Maine Historical Society: without your hard work and guidance, this book would have never been done.

To Allan M. Levinsky: it was an honor working with you on your great book *The Night the Sky Turned Red*. I learned so much as your chief researcher. As I ventured into this project, I knew that you would make the perfect co-writer with your additions to the historical pieces in the book, and taking on the job as the editor was more than I ever expected. Thank you, Allan!

To the staff of the Maine Historical Society: it is so much fun to work with such a great group of people every day.

To Katie Orlando, formerly of The History Press: it was a great pleasure working with you; your hard work and positive attitude made it happen. To Judie Percival and Herb Adams: thanks for the wonderful, heartfelt additions to the book. And of course, many thanks to Paul Flemming.

INTRODUCTION

In 1785, a former Revolutionary War general named Peleg Wadsworth decided to move his family to a small town on the coast of the Province of Maine, then part of Massachusetts, and go into business. He purchased one and a half acres of land facing a road called Back Street on the western end of the town called Falmouth.

He built a two-story brick house for his family with an attached building to be used as his place of business. In 1786, with the construction finally completed, Peleg; his wife, Elizabeth; and their large family moved in to begin their new lives. Among the children was a young lady named Zilpah who would become a key player in the Henry Wadsworth Longfellow story.

On January 1, 1804, Zilpah Wadsworth and Stephen Longfellow were married, and on February 27, 1807, their second child was born: a son they named Henry Wadsworth Longfellow. Born in a house on the waterfront, Henry and his family lived there a few months. Conveniently for the Longfellows, Peleg had also purchased 7,500 acres of land upstate in a small Maine town named Hiram. He had also built a house there and decided that he and his family would move there in 1807 to conduct a farming and lumbering business. He turned his Portland property over to his daughter and her family, who then moved in to what would become the Longfellow family home until the death of Henry's younger sister, Anne, in 1901.

In this book, you will dig deeply into the poet's life before he became famous around the world. The majority of historical biographers have concentrated on his later life and his poetry, overlooking the events of his early life. Here you will discover his development into the man he became as he graduated college, traveled through Europe and became a professor at both Bowdoin College and Harvard.

Through his many letters to his family and friends, you will experience, in his own words, his adventures and feelings about happenings in his young life. It is like being by his side with him as he travels from country to country and enlightens young students in the classroom.

Readers also have an additional benefit as they learn about Longfellow's formative years—exciting periods of Portland history during the time that young Longfellow was absent from his family and hometown. The city has grown considerably, both in physical size and population.

By 1825, on a lot in Monument Square just a short block from the Longfellow House, a new city hall was built. It was used not only as a place to conduct city business but also as a public market. The lower floors held shops that provided substantial revenue for Portland. By 1830, there were 1,076 houses, 280 stores for the sale of merchandise, 305 offices and shops, 119 warehouses and 8 factories.

Henry, upon his return to his home city, probably looked on with amazement at all the growth as he made ready to start his new life.

THE WADSWORTH-LONGFELLOW HOUSE is the oldest standing brick structure on the Portland peninsula that was on a site originally inhabited by the Native Americans, who named the town Machigonne. The name would be changed a number of times: in 1633, it changed to Casco; in 1658, it was changed to Falmouth; and in 1786, the year the Wadsworth-Longfellow House was finished, the citizens of Falmouth would form a separate town that they renamed Portland.

Portland became the capital in 1820, the year Maine became a state, and remained the capital until 1832. The Wadsworth-Longfellow House was the first historic site in Maine, and it was the boyhood home of the famous nineteenth-century poet Henry Wadsworth Longfellow.

The home was located on an acre and a half of land facing a road called Back Street, which the town's residents referred to as "the road that leads out of town." The house served three generations of Wadsworth and Longfellow family members until 1901.

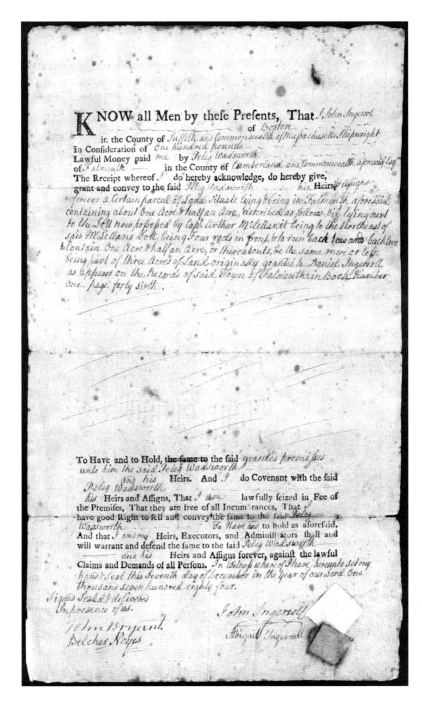

KNOW all Men by these Presents, That *John Ingersol*
of *Boston*
ir. the County of *Suffolk and Commonwealth of Massachusetts Shipwright*
In Consideration of *One hundred pounds*
Lawful Money paid *me* by *Peleg Wadsworth*
of *Falmouth* in the County of *Cumberland and commonwealth aforesaid Esq*
The Receipt whereof *I* do hereby acknowledge, do hereby give,
grant and convey to the said *Peleg Wadsworth* his Heirs *& assigns*
*forever a certain parcel of Land situate lying & being in Falmouth aforesaid
containing about One Acre & half an Acre, described as follows viz: lying next
to the Lott now possessed by Capt Arthur McLellan it being to the Northeast of
said McLellans Lott, being Four rods in front, & to run back four rods and back two
to contain One Acre & half an Acre, or thereabouts, be the same more or less.
being part of three Acres of Land originally granted to Daniel Ingersoll
as appears on the Records of said Town of Falmouth, in Book Number
One. page forty sixth.*

To Have and to Hold, ~~the same to~~ the said *granted premises*
unto him the said Peleg Wadsworth
and his Heirs. And *I* do Covenant with the said
Peleg Wadsworth
his Heirs and Assigns, That *I am* lawfully seized in Fee of
the Premises, That they are free of all Incumbrances, That *I*
have good Right to sell and convey the same to the said *Peleg
Wadsworth To have and* to hold as aforesaid.
And that *I am my* Heirs, Executors, and Administrators sha ll and
will warrant and defend the same to the said *Peleg Wadsworth*
and his Heirs and Assigns forever, against the lawful
Claims and Demands of all Persons. *In Witness where of I have hereunto set my
hand & seal this Seventh day of December in the Year of our Lord One
thousand seven hundred eighty four.*
*Signed Sealed & delivered
In presence of us.*
John Bryant. *John Ingersoll*
Belcher Noyes *Abigail Ingersoll*

Deed for land sold to Peleg Wadsworth from John Ingersoll in 1784. *Courtesy of the Collections of Maine Historical Society.*

Deed for land sold to Peleg Wadsworth from John Ingersoll in 1784, reverse side. *Courtesy of the Collections of Maine Historical Society.*

This section of town grew gradually. Soon new homes and shops were being built, and the small city continued to grow. But up through the Revolutionary War period, Back Street was the edge of the town. The city was attacked, bombarded and burned down on four different

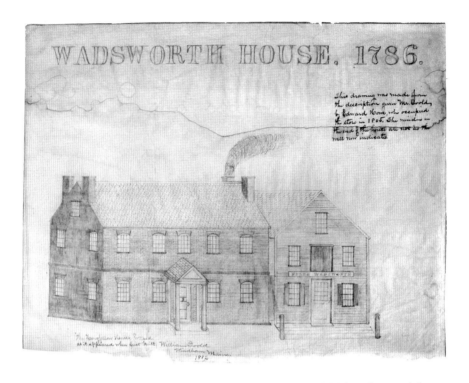

The home Peleg Wadsworth had built on Back Street in Portland, Maine. *Courtesy of the Collections of Maine Historical Society.*

Silhouette of Stephen Longfellow and wife Zilpah Wadsworth Longfellow. *Courtesy of the Collections of Maine Historical Society.*

Congress Street as it looked in 1800. *Courtesy of the Collections of Maine Historical Society.*

occasions—1676, 1690, 1775 and 1866. The phoenix, the mythical bird that rises from its ashes to live again, is the symbol of the city of Portland, and *resurgam*, the Latin word meaning "I shall rise again," is it's slogan.

Note: All misspellings and mistakes in the letters have been left just as they were when originally written to give the readers a sense of authenticity.

–ALLAN M. LEVINSKY

THE POET'S BIRTH

On February 27, 1807, the poet Henry Wadsworth Longfellow was born to father Stephen Longfellow and mother Zilpah Wadsworth Longfellow. At the time of the poet's birth, they were staying at Stephen's sister Abigail's home while her husband, Captain Samuel Stephenson, was away at sea. The home was located on the corner of Fore and Hancock Streets facing the harbor and remained there until it was torn down in the 1950s.

The year 1807 was also when the Portland Observatory was built in the area called Munjoy Hill on the east side of the town. In 1807, Portland, then part of Massachusetts, was a thriving seaport that had a problem. Merchants on the wharfs did not know what ships were expected to dock or at what time, so rounding up manpower needed to unload the cargo became a big problem. Captain Lemuel Moody, a sea captain and Portland resident, came up with a solution. He would build an observatory overlooking the harbor. Using signal flags, the observatory could help the merchants identify vessels so they could reserve wharf space and hire the manpower they would need to get the cargo unloaded.

By June 1812, the British Royal Navy had impressed more than six thousand of our seamen, and the U.S. government had had it. On June 18, 1812, Congress declared war against England. Much of the war passed Portland by except for one famous incident that took place about forty miles from the town on September 6, 1813, when a sixteen-gun British brig, HMS *Boxer*, began firing on an American privateer, the brig *Margaretta*. When the news reached Portland, it was noticed by the captain of the USS *Enterprise*,

The birthplace of the poet Henry Wadsworth Longfellow. *Courtesy of the Collections of Maine Historical Society.*

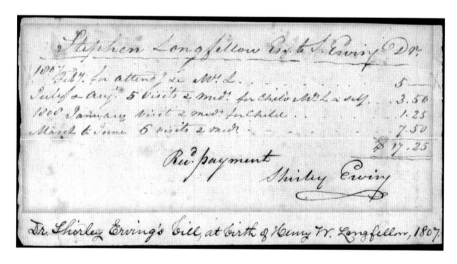

Doctor's bill for Henry Wadsworth Longfellow's birth, 1807. *Courtesy of the Collections of Maine Historical Society.*

anchored in Portland Harbor, and he immediately made his way to engage the British ship. He reached it by 5:00 a.m., and shots were engaged. The battle was engaged until 3:45 p.m. During the battle, a large crowd gathered at the observatory to see the smoke from the cannon fire, the only evidence that war had come to the area.

Benj.ᵈ Goold of Windham agrees to furnish Jonᵈ Stuart & others with eight sticks of pine timber of sixty five feet in length, fourteen inches square at the butt & ten inches at the top to be delivered on the Common near the Neck in Portland by the first may at the price of twelve dollars for stick, to be paid when delivered and other timber as we agree hereafter agree on —

Portland April 8th 1807

Above: Observatory timber contract, Portland, 1807. *Courtesy of the Collections of Maine Historical Society.*

Right: Raising of the Portland Monument, 1807. The names of the people who helped to construct the Portland Observatory. *Courtesy of the Collection of Maine Historical Society.*

In 1807, the population of Portland was six thousand people. In December of that year, Thomas Jefferson imposed an embargo on trade. As a result, American exports dropped from $108 million in 1807 to $22 million in 1808. The embargo had a lasting and damaging impact on Maine. Prior to the embargo, Portland was one of the most prosperous cities in New England. But by early 1808, many of the leading Portland ship owners and merchants had failed, and unemployment in coastal towns had risen close to 60 percent. Portland's leading residents established a soup kitchen for the unemployed, providing one free soup dinner per day for out-of-work men and their families. The Embargo Act of 1807 lasted until March 1809, effectively halting American overseas trade. The United States suffered greatly, and in the commercial parts of New England, ships sat at the wharves to rot. It was a financial disaster for America because the British were still able to export goods here.

During this time, Maine remained loyal to the Republican Party while most of Massachusetts did not. Some residents were driven by hard times and had to resort to smuggling to earn a living, and Maine became one of the most notorious areas for illegal trade with Canada. Despite the economic troubles plaguing Portland and the young nation, Stephen Longfellow's business thrived and provided a comfortable life for the family.

Henry Wadsworth Longfellow's childhood was a pleasant one, with very nurturing and understanding parents and a very close relationship with his siblings. Portland was a seaport town, and much of the poetry Henry wrote came back to the town he so loved. From the front of the second floor of his childhood home, he could look out at Portland Harbor and see as far as Portland Head, home of the lighthouse in Cape Elizabeth. His poem "The Lighthouse" is known to have been written in Longfellow's childhood home:

> *The Rocky ledge runs far into the sea,*
> *And on its outer point, some miles away,*
> *The Lighthouse lifts its massive masonry,*
> *A pillar of fire by night, of cloud by day.*
>
> *Even at this distance I can see the tides,*
> *Upheaving, break unheard along its base,*
> *A speechless wrath, that rises and subsides*
> *In the white lip and tremor of the face.*

And as the evening darkens, lo! How bright,
*   Through the deep purple of the twilight air,*
Beams forth the sudden radiance of its light
*   With strange, unearthly splendor in the glare!*

Not one alone; from each projecting cape
*   And the perilous reef along the ocean's verge,*
Starts into life a dim, gigantic shape,
*   Holding its lantern o'er the restless surge.*

Like a great giant Christopher it stands
*   Upon the brink of the tempestuous wave,*
Wading far out among the rocks and sands,
*   The night-o'rtaken mariner to save.*

And the great ships sail outward and return,
*   Bending and bowing o'er the billowy swells,*
And ever joyful, as they see it burn,
*   They wave their silent welcomes and farewells.*

They come forth from the darkness, and their sails
*   Gleam for a moment only in the blaze,*
And eager faces, as the light unveils,
*   Gaze at the tower, and vanish while they gaze.*

From the back of the home, Henry could see the White Mountains of New Hampshire. Deering Woods was on the western part of town, where the poet enjoyed the beautiful natural scenery, reading under the trees and bathing in the creek. He remembered the days in the poem "My Lost Youth":

And Deering's Woods are fresh and fair,
*   And with joy that is almost pain*
My heart goes back to wander there,
*   And among the dreams of the days that were,*
I find my lost youth again.
*   And the strange and beautiful song,*
The groves are repeating still:
*   "A boy's will is the wind's will,*
And thoughts of youth are long, long thoughts."

Commemorative pitcher of the Portland Observatory, drawing with signals numbered and an explanation, 1807. *Courtesy of the Collections of Maine Historical Society.*

A watercolor of the Portland Observatory and the twenty-four signal flags used to let merchants know when their vessels were entering Portland Harbor. This watercolor is attributed to Lemuel Moody, circa 1807. *Courtesy of the Collections of Maine Historical Society.*

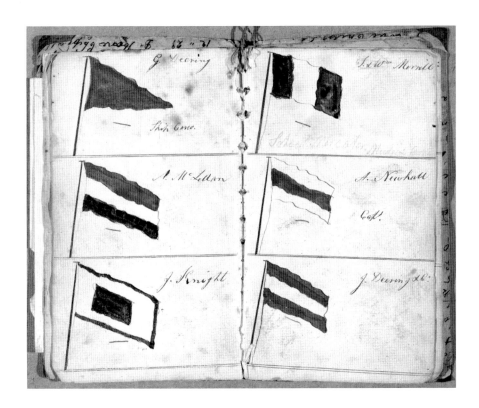

Above: Six signal flags for ship owners used at the Portland Observatory. The observatory on Munjoy Hill (or Mountjoy Neck) raised the appropriate flag to communicate the arrival of ships in Portland Harbor, circa 1810. *Courtesy of the Collections of Maine Historical Society.*

Right: Four lunettes depict views of Portland and vicinity from Casco Bay. The views are bordered with signal flags of Portland merchants, 1807. *Courtesy of the Collections of Maine Historical Society.*

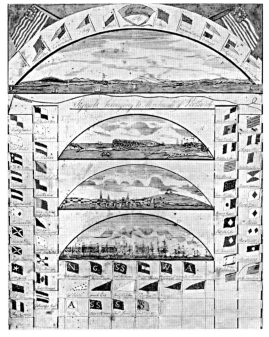

Portland Observatory subscriber agreement, 1807. *Courtesy of the Collections of Maine Historical Society.*

To the east of the home was Munjoy Hill. This area consisted of open fields and pastures, but on the Fore Street end of the hill, there was a very busy seaport with wharves and schooners; at the top of Munjoy Hill, there was the eighty-six-foot-tall Portland Observatory. It still stands today, overlooking the harbor.

Henry's father was a lawyer, and as part of his practice, he traveled throughout Maine, attending court sessions, spending time away from his young family. In a very early letter, Zilpah wrote to her husband, Stephen, who was away, of young Henry: "I think you would like my Henry W. He is an active rogue, and wishes for nothing so much as singing and dancing."

Henry also had a close relationship with both of his grandparents, spending part of his summers in Gorham, Maine, at his grandfather Judge Stephen Longfellow's home and in Hiram, Maine, with his grandfather Peleg Wadsworth at his home. Judge Stephen Longfellow was born in Gorham and was a leading citizen of the town, serving as a representative and senator in the Massachusetts legislature and as a judge. General Peleg Wadsworth was born in Duxbury, Massachusetts, a Revolutionary War hero who had been wounded, taken prisoner, escaped

Left: Silhouette of Peleg Wadsworth. *Courtesy of Collections of the Maine Historical Society.*

Rgiht: Silhouette of Elizabeth Bartlett Wadsworth. *Courtesy of the Collections of Maine Historical Society.*

and continued to fight the British encroachment of the Northeast. He participated in the government of Portland and was elected as a senator in the Massachusetts legislature.

Life for the children was a very happy one at the childhood home. The poet's younger sister, Anne, remembered, "Books and satchels were the ornaments of the parlor table in the evening, and silence the motto, till lessons were learned—then fun and games were not wanting, and when they grew too fast...for the parlor, the old kitchen rang with our shouts and glee."

Also living in the childhood home was Aunt Lucia, Zilpah's younger sister, who helped raise all eight Longfellow children. The children had a saying they would recite to tell folks their name in the order of their birth: "Stephen and Henry, Elizabeth and Anne, Alex and Mary, Ellen and Sam."

From the poem "Musings," known to have been written in Longfellow's childhood home, comes the following:

> *I sat by my window one night,*
> *And watched how the stars grew high;*
> *And the earth and skies were a splendid sight*
> *To a sober and musing eye*
>
> *From heaven the silver moon shone down*
> *With gentle and mellow ray,*
> *And beneath the crowded roofs of the town*
> *In broad light and shadow lay.*
>
> *A glory was on the silent sea,*
> *And mainland and island too,*
> *Till a haze came over the lowland lea,*
> *And shrouded that beautiful blue.*

THE POET AND THE WAR OF 1812

The War of 1812 started on June 18, when young Henry was only five years old, and lasted until February 18, 1815, just nine days before Henry's eighth birthday. In a letter, Zilpah wrote of young Henry: "He was prepared to march against the British at a moment's notice," and that his tin gun had been ready for a week. At the time of the war, he would write to his father from the home in Portland: "Ann wants a little bible like Betsy's. Will you please buy her one if you can find any in Boston. I have been to school all week and got seven marks. I shall have a billet on Monday. I wish you to buy me a drum." Henry's mother, Zilpah, wrote to her husband, who was in Boston attending the General Court: "Enclosed is Henry's letter, the product of some hours attentive employment. I mention this that you may appreciate it not by it's appearance but by it's intrinsic value." Stephen responded to the letter, writing to Henry that he had found a drum with an eagle painted on it and that he would purchase the drum if he could find a way to send it to Portland. At the time of the letters, no ships were being allowed to sail from Boston to Portland due to the war.

On September 5, 1813, a battle between the British brig *Boxer* and USS *Enterprise* began off Monhegan and Seguin Island, Maine. When the fighting was finally over, the *Enterprise* was the victor and the *Boxer* lay in ruins. Both ships were damaged badly in the battle, with the *Enterprise* suffering damage to the rigging, while the *Boxer* suffered damage in its rigging, hull and mast, making it very difficult to keep it afloat as it was towed back into Portland. In this battle, the commander of the *Boxer*, twenty-nine-year-old captain

Henry Wadsworth Longfellow in 1815, by artist William Hendrik Franquinet,
The portrait is on ivory with a blue felt interior in a period brass frame, 1840.
Courtesy of the Collections of Maine Historical Society.

Samuel Blyth, died during the opening exchange of cannon fire. Command
of the *Boxer* was taken over by Lieutenant David McGrery. *Boxer* casualties
totaled seven killed and thirteen wounded.

Mortally wounded a short time later during this battle was *Enterprise* captain
William Burrows, age twenty-eight. Command of the *Enterprise* was assumed
by Lieutenant Edward McCall. *Enterprise* casualties were four killed and ten
wounded. The dying Lieutenant Burrows declined to accept Commander

Blyth's sword. "I am satisfied, I die contented," he said, asking that the sword be sent to the family of Blyth. In later years, Longfellow would recount the battle and the military honors given to the captains in the poem "My Lost Youth":

> *I remember the sea-fight far away,*
> *How it thundered o'er the tide!*
> *And the dead captains, as they lay*
> *In their graves, o'erlooking the tranquil bay,*
> *Where they in battle died.*
> *And the sound of that mournful song*
> *Goes through me with a thrill:*
> *"A boy's will is the wind's will,*
> *And the thoughts of youth are long, long thoughts."*

A state funeral was conducted for the two commanders, who lay at rest side by side in the Eastern Cemetery on Congress Street in Portland, not far from the poet's boyhood home. In a tribute of respect to Captain Blyth, the gravestone was placed at his grave by the crew of the *Boxer*. Blyth's mahogany coffin and trimmings cost twenty-four dollars, and burial cost was eleven dollars. Also laying at rest next to the captains is Kervin Waters. Wounded in the battle, Waters died about two years later on September 25,

Battle between the *Boxer* and the *Enterprise*, September 5, 1813. *Courtesy of the Collections of Maine Historical Society.*

31

Artist Charles Frederick Kimball depicts the graves of Lieutenant William Burrows, captain of the USS *Enterprise*, and Captain Samuel Blyth, commander of the HMS *Boxer*. *Courtesy of the Collections of Maine Historical Society.*

1815. He was rewarded for his bravery with the commission of lieutenant. Waters would live to see the end of the War of 1812. A broadside about the end of war read:

> *"PEACE CONCLUDED—LET ALL THE PEOPLE THANK GOD, AND SAY AMEN!*
>
> *THE Committee appointed at a full meeting of the Inhabitants of this town, to adopt suitable measures for a general expression of joy on the return of PEACE, having learned officially the cessation of Hostilities, and the ratification of a TREATY OF PEACE, have recommended, that the dawn of this day be welcomed by a National Salute from the Forts in town, and Bells be rung one hour, beginning at sunrise…That Military companies in town turn out, and fire a fue-de-joie under the direction of Major STORER.*
>
> *And that Col. STARK, the Commander of this Military post, be requested to join the People of the town and country in celebrating this joyful event by firing a Grand Salute from the Forts under his command. That at noon, national Salutes be fired under the direction of Major WEEKS, and the bells be rung from 12 to 1 o'clock…and one hour before sun-down…and*

the day closed with another National Salute.—That in the evening such of the Inhabitants as can conveniently, will illuminate the windows of their dwelling-houses, to begin with the ringing of the bells at half-past seven, and the lights put out when the bells shall cease, at nine o'clock.

The committee also recommended, that good order be observed, and that houses not illuminated may be attributed to inconvenience or not being occupied. And that the Selectmen appoint a Constable's watch of 24, to guard the town against fire, & preserve order....No bonfires to be allowed in the streets or lanes in town; and it would be well if none were kindled… and the people retire to their dwellings at an early hour.

By order of the Committee,   Daniel Tucker, *Chairman.*

"Banish discord…Peace we'll cherish!
War has ceas'd…may Commerce flourish!"
Portland, February 1815.

Henry was attending a private school by the end of the war, kept by Nathaniel Hazeltine Carter, a Dartmouth graduate. This was not Henry's first school. When he was only three years old, he and older brother, Stephen, attended a school on Spring Street in Portland kept by Ma'am Fellows.

Henry also went to a public school for a short time on Center Street and then went to Mr. Wright's private school and on to the Portland Academy with Mr. N.H. Carter and Mr. Bezaleel Cushman. In 1813, Cushman sent a billet to Stephen and Zipah, writing, "Master Henry Longfellow is one of the best boys we have in school. He spells and reads very well. He also can add and multiply numbers. His conduct last quarter was very correct and amiable." On November 1, 1817, Cushman sent a billet on the progress of the two brothers Stephen and Henry, stating, "Mr. Longfellow Sir: Stephen & Henry have both commenced this quarter with an unusual degree diligence in their studies—Their deportment also is remarkably good—Yours very respectfully B. Cushman." Henry attended the Portland Academy until 1821 and graduated at age fourteen.

At the time the Longfellow boys were attending Mr. Cater and Mr. Bezaleel's Portland Academy, the city of Portland was growing, and the fear of fire was always on the minds of its residents. Twice, fire had affected the Longfellows. In 1814, Stephen's law office sustained a fire, requiring him to move his office into the home, where the dining/sitting room was located. A

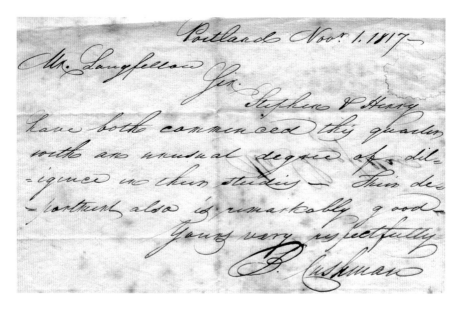

School report on Stephen and Henry Wadsworth Longfellow, 1817. *Courtesy of the Collections of Maine Historical Society.*

second fire in the kitchen fireplace badly burned the roof of the house. As a result of the fire damage, and with the family continuing to grow, the idea for a third-floor addition was put into practice, changing the façade of the building to resemble a Federal-style home. While repairs were being finished after the fire at the Portland home, Henry wrote a letter to his father from his grandparents' home, where he was staying with his mother, Zilpah:

HIRAM, AUGUST 1815

Dear Papa, I wish you would tell me in your next letter how the house comes on. And I wish you would bring me a Childs Companion, for Charles Wadsworth. I do not know but I have one at home, but if you buy one I can pay you again. I believe it will cost only nine pence. I thank you for those books you sent me. I have read the riddle book through and learnt several riddles. I like the stories in the other book very well.

Earlier that year, on April 22, 1815, a notification for the appointment of fire wards was released to let the people of the city know who was named as wards, as well as the responsibilities that were included in this position. Stephen Longfellow was appointed as a ward, along with a number of other men for that year. Also in Portland in 1815, the Maine Charitable Mechanic Association was founded with the goal of promoting excellence among Portland's artistic and mechanical trades, including sail makers, shipbuilders, brick masons, stonecutters, watchmakers and nautical instrument makers. Furniture makers and similar craftsmen also learned their skills and crafts through apprenticeship education sponsored by the Maine Charitable Mechanics Association. The organization's library was started in 1820. Apart from the new businesses and organizations that were opening in the town, fire continued to be the subject of conversation among the residents of Portland, demonstrated in this next passage from a historic document called "The Fire Wards of Portland" dated January 6, 1818:

> *Anxious to preserve the town from the horrors of conflagration, are induced again to address their Fellow Citizens on that interesting and important subject. Vigilance and carefulness are at all times indispensible duties of every citizen, but they are peculiarly so at this inclement season, when the danger of fire is so great and the consequences so alarming and distressing.—Wholesome regulations, on this subject, have been adopted by the town, and the Fire Wards are pledged to see them faithfully and rigourously enforced.—But our best exertions will prove ineffectual, if the inhabitants are inattentive to their duties, and regardless of their own safety or the security of others.—As the vigilance and attention of a few will be vain and ineffectual, while others are careless and inattentive, it is the duty of every individual to guard against that carelessness and those accidents by which fires are generally communicated.*
>
> *Permit us therefore earnestly to solicit your attention to those measures of precaution, which have been so often urged upon you, and which are essential to the security of the town; and also to caution you against those careless habits from which most of the calamities of fire have proceeded.—Particularly would we notice the dangerous habit of carrying candles and lamps into stables and wood-houses without being secured in lanterns.—Saving ashes in wood vessels, and placing them in cellars and out-houses before the fire is entirely extinguished—putting away brooms, which have been used in the evening, without immersing them in water—leaving wood un-extinguished in fire-places and stoves—smoking cigars in the streets, stables and out-houses—and the dangerous habit which prevails among some, of reading by candle-light, after they retired to bed. We would also recommend a particular attention to your chimneys, stoves and ovens to see that they are in good order, and in every respect safe—on cabinet-makers, the utmost care and caution—the nature of their employments, even with the greatest care, must ever expose them and*

their neighbors to danger, but with care, ruin is inevitable.—A moment's carelessness may destroy the hard earnings of a whole life, and involve hundreds in distress. Let us all remember the horror, confusion, dismay and ruin, which have been occasioned by inattention to these things; and by the recollection of past misfortunes, may we learn to avoid future calamities.

While Stephen was traveling away from Portland for business and political affairs in Wiscasset and Augusta, Maine, in the fall of 1820, Dr. Samuel Weed was attending to Stephen's wife, Zilpah, who was very ill at the time. The following letters from Henry to his father address his mother's health and other topics concerning the family.

PORTLAND SEPTEMBER 15ᵀᴴ 1820

Dear Sir

Perhaps you are impatient to hear from us and to know how mama's health is and I now take my pen to inform you that she is better than the Doctor expected she would be at this time. This evening while I was studying my Greek, Elizabeth wrote you a letter but making some mistakes in directing it and being called for by mama, she had not time enough to finish another, and I, thinking you would wish to hear from us, took this opportunity to write you this short letter, in haste, as you will see by the writing. It is now twenty-five minutes past eight, and I am sitting in the parlour with Alexander by me almost asleep—he hangs his head upon his shoulder. Poor little boy, he wants to go to bed! A minute or two ago I called him by name—he only raised his head and without opening his eyes answered "what." Stephen is just carrying him up to bed and so, if you please, I will wish you a good night.

Henry W Longfellow

PORTLAND, MONDAY, SEPTEMBER 25 1820

Dear Sir

Doctor thinks mama is better to night. She set up an hour and a half to day. Instead of keeping my money until tomorrow to spend in "trifles" I thought it would be better to buy books with it and accordingly I bought two "plays." I don't much think I shall go over to the plains tomorrow but stay in town and take a little bit of a ride on horse back.

Grand-papa Wadsworth arrived here from Hiram this evening. You must excuse the shortness of this letter and "badness of the writing" which is owing to my not having a good pen—and not having a sharp knife I am not able to make a better one.

Henry W. Longfellow

PORTLAND OCTOBER 8ᵀᴴ 1820

Dear Sir

Mama thinks she has not amended much, for the week past, and therefor says you must expect to find her very smart. A letter was received from, "your humble servant" Mr. Joseph Pierce, of Boston, from which I have made an extract which contains all that will be necessary for you to know, as the other part of the letter contains nothing of business nor importance. He says that he is apprehensive that his letter of the 21ˢᵗ of September was not sufficiently explicit. And further that "On recurring to the copy, it appears that you might perhaps consider yourself as retained for the Twenty Associates only in the case now pending—whereas I wished it to be understood that you were retained in all cases, wherein the Twenty Associates are, or may be a party, either directly or indirectly, in any suits now commenced, or may be thereafter commenced, by then or against them. Therefore if you did not so understand it before—please consider it in that light now—and confirm it accordingly." We received an other letter to day (Sunday) from Mr. Mark L Hill Jun (Philipsburgh) enclosing five dollars which Wm. Davis handed him wishing him to enclose it to you, for B. Adams who Requested him to inform you that he will send the remainder in a few day—says that he should have sent it before but was disappointed in getting it.

I like Mr. Cobbs, as a preceptor, as well as any one I ever had. He seems to understand the languages so well, that nothing appears to perplex him, but on the contrary, he answers all our questions with as much quickness and facility as if he had just received them (the languages).

Stephen wishes to sell you, his elegant watch, which has been lately fixed and now keeps very good time. He offers it for six dollars, which he thinks cheap enough, considering the "repairs" it has undergone which, if you buy the watch, he intends to pay for. (per order). An address will be delivered before the Portland Benevolent Society, on Wednesday evening next, by John. P.B. Storer—Esq—at which I purpose to attend.

Henry W. Longfellow

While Stephen Longfellow was traveling for both business and political affairs, the letters from his young son Henry helped Stephen to keep abreast of the mother's health. Postwar momentum for statehood continued to grow, and Stephen, aware of the need for statehood and the separation from Massachusetts, would go on to become a delegate at the Maine Constitution Convention.

THE POET AND STATEHOOD

In October 1819, the Maine Constitution Convention was held at First Parish Meetinghouse, and the Maine Constitution was approved by all 210 of the delegates. The Maine Constitution was approved by Congress on March 4, 1820, as part of the Missouri Compromise, which offered balance between the northern free states and southern pro slave states. The northern states approved the statehood of Missouri, which was a slave state, in exchange for Maine's statehood (being a free state).

The proclamation reads:

> *Whereas the delegates of the people of Maine assemble in Convention at Portland by adjournment on the fifth day of January last, Resolved that after fifteenth day of March, than next, on condition that the proposed State of Maine shall have been admitted into the Union, the President be requested to issue his Proclamation to the people of the State of Maine, making known such admission, and that the Constitution proposed by the Convention and adopted by the People is the Constitution and frame of government for the State. Now therefore, I, William King, President of the Convention aforesaid, do by these presents make known, that on the third day of March instant the State of Maine was by an Act of Congress of the United States of America admitted into the Union on an equal footing with the original States from and after the fifteenth day of March instant, and that the Constitution prepared by said Convention and by them submitted to the People, was adopted by the People, and is now the Constitution and frame of Government of the State of Maine—of all which, the citizens of said state will take notice and govern themselves accordingly.*

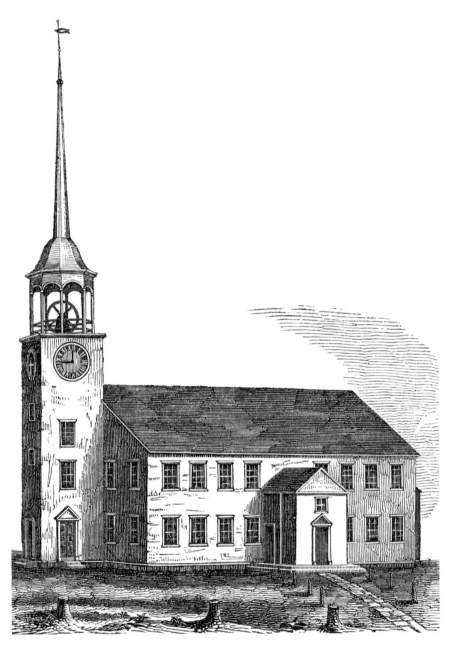

First Parish Meetinghouse was known as "Old Jerusalem." This engraving shows the first church established in Portland (then Falmouth), circa 1821. *Courtesy of the Collections of Maine Historical Society.*

STATE OF MAINE.

By WILLIAM KING,

President of the Convention,

A PROCLAMATION.

WHEREAS the delegates of the People of Maine assembled in Convention at Portland by adjournment on the fifth day of January last, Resolved "that after the fifteenth day of March, then next, on condition that the " proposed State of Maine shall have been admitted into the Union, the " President be requested to issue his Proclamation to the People of the " State of Maine, making known such admission, and that the Constitution " proposed by the Convention and adopted by the People, is the Constitution " and frame of government for the State." Now therefore, I, WILLIAM KING, President of the Convention aforesaid, do by these presents make known, that on the third day of March instant the State of Maine was by an Act of the Congress of the United States of America admitted into the Union on an equal footing with the original States from and after the fifteenth day of March instant; and that the Constitution prepared by said Convention and by them submitted to the People, was adopted by the People, and is now the Constitution and frame of Government of the State of Maine—of all which the citizens of said State will take notice and govern themselves accordingly.

Done at Portland, this sixteenth day of March, in the year of our Lord one thousand eight hundred and twenty, and of the Independence of the United States the forty-fourth.

WILLIAM KING.

By the President of the Convention,

ASHUR WARE, *Secretary of State pro tem.*

Proclamation of statehood, 1820. *Courtesy of the Collections of Maine Historical Society.*

Done at Portland, this sixteenth day of March, in the year of our Lord one thousand eight hundred and twenty, and of the Independence of the United States the forty-fourth.

William King

By the President of the Convention
Ashur Ware, Secretary of State pro tem.

Thomas Jefferson's letter to William King, 1819. *Courtesy of the Collections of Maine Historical Society.*

Stephen Longfellow was one of the 210 delegates in attendance at the convention. Maine became the twenty-third state in the Union on March 15; it was no longer a part of Massachusetts.

William King from Bath, Maine, was chosen as the state's first governor, and Portland became Maine's first capital. The first president of the Maine state Senate was William D. Williamson, and when Governor King resigned from the governorship in 1821, Williamson succeeded him.

Thomas Jefferson wrote a letter to William King in response to receiving a copy of the Maine Constitution, dated November 17, 1819. The letter reads:

> *Th. Jefferson returns thanks to General King for his kind communication of the constitution of Maine, which finds marked with wisdom in every point, except that of representation. Equal representation is so fundamental a principle in a true republic that no prejudices can justify it's [sic] violation because the prejudice themselves cannot be justified. The claims of the corporate towns in this case, like those of the barons in England have forced the body of the nation to accept a government by capitulation, these equal rights of the people at large are forced to yield to the privileges of a few. However, you will amend it by and by. In the mean time I welcome the new state into our union and salute General King with the most friendly recollections and assurances of esteem and respect.*
>
> *Monticello, Nov. 19. 19.*

THE POET AND COLLEGE

In the Portland home, at the age of thirteen, Henry Wadsworth Longfellow wrote a poem called "The Battle of Lovell's Pond," a story that he remembered his grandfather Peleg Wadsworth would tell him on his visits to his home in Hiram, Maine. The location of the battle took place not far from the Hiram home in 1725.

The work is the first published poem by the young poet who only signed "Henry" at the bottom of the piece, which appeared in the local newspaper called the *Portland Gazette*. The story of the poem is that on the evening of the publication, Henry was visiting at the home of schoolmate Frederic Mellen. Frederic's father, Judge Mellen, commented about the poem, calling it "[v]ery stiff, remarkably stiff; moreover, it is all borrowed, every word of it." The comments of the judge did not settle well with the poet, but he did not let on to the judge that he was author of the said stiff and borrowed poem. Later, he asked his mother, Zilpah, to read the poem for her honest opinion.

The *Portland Gazette* piece reads:

> *Poetry. For the Gazette. THE BATTLE OF LOVELL'S POND. Cold, cold is the north wind, and rude is the blast, That sweeps, like a hurricane, loudly and fast, As it moans through the tall waving pines, lone and drear, Sighs a requiem, sad, o'er the warrior's bier. The war—whoop is still, and the savage's yell Has sunk into silence, along the wild dell: The din of the battle, the tumult, is o'er, And the war—clarion's voice is now heard no more. The warriors that fought for their country, and*

bled, Have sunk to their rest; the damp earth is their bed, No stone tells the place where their ashes repose, Nor points out the spot from the graves of their foes. They proclaim; They are dead; but they live in each Patriot's breast, And their names are engraved on honor's bright crest. Henry.

A similar poem by Thomas C. Upham called "Lovellspond" appear in a collection of Upham's called *American Sketches*.

In 1821, Henry graduated from the Portland Academy at the age of fourteen. Stephen and young Henry then enrolled at Bowdoin College in Brunswick, Maine. Stephen was sixteen. In 1821, Portland High School was

Drawing of the Wadsworth-Longfellow House in Portland, donated to the Maine Historical Society by Anne Longfellow Pierce. *Courtesy of the Collections of Maine Historical Society.*

POETRY.

For the Gazette.

THE BATTLE OF LOVELL'S POND.

COLD, cold is the north-wind, and rude is the
    blast,
That sweeps, like a hurricane, loudly and fast,
As it moans through the tall waving pines, lone
    and drear,
Sighs a requiem, sad, o'er the warrior's bier.

The war-whoop is still, and the savage's yell
Has sunk into silence, along the wild dell ;
The din of the battle, the tumult, is o'er,
And the war-clarion's voice is now heard no more.

The warriors that fought for their country—and
    bled,
Have sunk to their rest ; the damp earth is their
    bed,
No stone tells the place where their ashes repose,
Nor points out the spot, from the graves of their
    foes.

They died in their glory surrounded by fame,
And Victory's loud trump their death did pro-
    claim.
They are dead ; but they live in each Patriot's
    breast,
And their names are engraven on honour's bright
    crest.   HENRY.

"The Battle of Lovell's Pond." *Courtesy of the Collections of Maine Historical Society.*

A sketch of the Wadsworth-Longfellow House on Congress Street in Portland portrays the house as it was in March 1821. *Courtesy of the Collections of Maine Historical Society.*

established, originally as a boys' school. The Cumberland and Oxford Canal was chattered by local merchants but would not open until 1832.

Henry's parents, Stephen and Zilpah, felt that Henry was much too young for college life and living away from home, so they made arrangements with Bowdoin College for the two boys to remain in Portland for their freshman year of college, along with their neighbors' son Edward "Ned" Preble. The three of them would be tutored by their old Portland Academy schoolmaster Bezaleel Cushman. In the fall of 1822, Stephen and a fifteen-year-old Henry arrived in Brunswick, Maine, along with Ned Preble, to begin their second year of studies at Bowdoin College. The dormitory, Maine Hall, could hold only 50 students of the 120 boys attending that year. Their father made arrangements for Henry and Stephen and their friend Ned to stay with Reverend Benjamin Titcomb. The rooms in winter were cold, and the fireplace was the only source of heat. Henry made a request to his sisters in Portland to make him some curtains to cover the drafty windows and provide some art for the walls. Henry also wrote to Stephen and Zilpah, describing college life:

BRUNSWICK SEPTEMBER 22ND 1822

Dear Parents,

As we have now got comfortably settled, I suppose it is about time to let you know how we go on here. I feel very contented, and am much pleased with College Life. Many of the students are very agreeable companions and, thus far, I have passed my time very pleasantly. The students have considerably more leisure than I expected, but as the season advances and the days grow shorter, our leisure moments must necessarily be considerably diminished. I expected, when I got here that I should have to study very hard to keep a good footing with the rest of the class; but I find I have sufficient time for the preparation of my lessons and for amusement, and that I am not more deficient than some of the rest of the class. I have not been screwed at recitation yet and shall endeavour not to be.

So much for egotism!

I have very little more to write, but I will not to forget to mention that by some means or other, I cannot tell what, I have either lost on my passage here, or left at home, all my cotton stockings except the one pair which I wore—and another thing is that I wish some one would get a brass ferrule put on to my cane and send it to me as soon as possible. If you have any good apples or pears I wish you would send me some—and tell the girls to send a whole parcel of Ginger bread with them. My box of tooth powder may also be put into the bundle.

Your's affectionately,
H.W.L.—

P.S. There is another thing of considerable importance, which I had like to have forgotten.
You do not know how much we stand in need of a good Watch. When the chapel bell rings for recitation it is only struck a few times and then is done, so that we, living so far from the College Building, are liable to be

Postcard of the house where Henry Wadsworth Longfellow roomed while a student at Bowdoin College in Brunswick, Maine. *Courtesy of the Collections of Maine Historical Society.*

late—however we must do the best we can. Give my love to all and tell the Girls to write soon.

The boys had to be at the college for 6:00 a.m. prayers and then their first recitation before they could return to the home of Reverend Benjamin Titcomb for breakfast.

The year 1822 is also when the Maine Historical Society was founded, making it the third oldest in the country. Massachusetts is the oldest, founded in 1792. New York is the second-oldest historical society, founded in 1804. Stephen Longfellow, along with Court Justice Prentiss Mellen and Governor William King, were all founding members of the Maine Historical Society. In later years, father Stephen would serve as the Maine Historical Society president and Henry Wadsworth Longfellow as the society's librarian.

In this next letter from December 1822, Henry writes to his mother about the cold days and nights. Not mentioned in this letter was that at one time, during a cold spell, Henry felt as though he was not getting enough exercise. So, drawing an image on the door, Henry would put on his boxing gloves and spar at the figure for exercise:

BOWDOIN COLLEGE. DECEMBER 7, 1822

My Dear Mother,

I received your letter of Novr 26—as returning from church, last Sunday. And now see what a scurvy trick Fortune (or rather Misfortune) has played me. The reason of my silence concerning our return at Thank{s}-giving was, that I wished to take you by surprise—and therefore said nothing, but kept you in doubt. You see how it ends. We are disappointed in our mode of conveyance and forced to remain. And there in lies the rub. I do not know when I have passed a week so unpleasantly or when time has lagged so much or hung so heavily upon my hands. First, the disappointment was a serious evil: added to this the long succession of cold days and cold nights—frozen ears—cold feet and a thousand other "ills the flesh is heir to"—all these make it dull living in this dreary region of the East. Heigh-ho for vacation. We ate our Thanksgiving dinner at Professor Cleaveland's; the professor was very sociable but I had rather by half have dined at home. I am very sorry to hear that Betsey has been indisposed and hope she has quite recovered again. I have not got well yet and what is more, do not see prospect of "a speedy recovery." However I make two meals on "pudding and milk," that is one good thing! We have fixed our fire-place as you mentioned. I think it may be advantageous as it respects warming the room, but the chimney is more inclined to smoke and that, you know, is about as disagreeable as cold is—but to have both is rather too bad. You say you can excuse the shortness of the letters. Be so kind as to excuse the shortness of mine! My love to all.

Your affectionate son
Henry.

PS. The letters I received by Mellen and Preble, I shall answer soon.

Classmates Frederic Mellen and Ned Preble brought the letters from Portland after returning from the Thanksgiving holiday.

Henry and Stephen returned to Portland for the next school break. While on the midterm holiday, Henry wrote a letter to his classmate Cullen Sawtelle of Norridgewock, Maine, remarking how

the two week have spilt rapidly away and agreeable too—the particulars when we meet again. An evening or two ago I had the pleasure of seeing a sketch of your beautiful village of Norridgewock—and I assure you I was greatly delighted with it. If it is in reality as beautiful and pleasant as it seemed from that sketch to be, it is just such a village as I should like to live—die—and be buried in. I know nothing so delightful as retiring from the smoke, noise, and dust of the town to the green fields of the country—tho' many prefer the town— noisy and dusty as it is. I feel pretty confident that life would wear smoothly away—with me—could I dwell in a neat country-house—upon the borders of some lake or river in the enjoyment of rural retirement—but this is mere talk!!

But Portland in 1823 was changing, as the poet wrote to his friend: "A new and correct plan of Portland, 1823 is drawn and engraved by Abel Bowen, this map shows the names of the streets, buildings, wharves, and the rope walks of Portland." Henry also wrote about the ropewalk in a poem:

FROM "THE ROPEWALK"

*In that building, long and low,
With its windows all a-row
Like the port-holes of a hulk,
Human spiders spin and spin,
Backward down their threads so thin
Dropping, each hempen bulk.*

*At the end, an open door:
Squares of sunshine on the floor
Light the long and dusky lane;
And the whirring of a wheel,
Dull and drowsy, makes me feel
All its spokes are in my brain.*

*As the spinners to the end
Downward go and reascend,
Gleam the long threads in the sun;
While within this brain of mine
Cobwebs brighter and more fine
By the busy wheel are spun.*

Portland's first Irish organization was formed in 1823, called the Roman Catholic Society according to the Portland City Directory. The great Irish

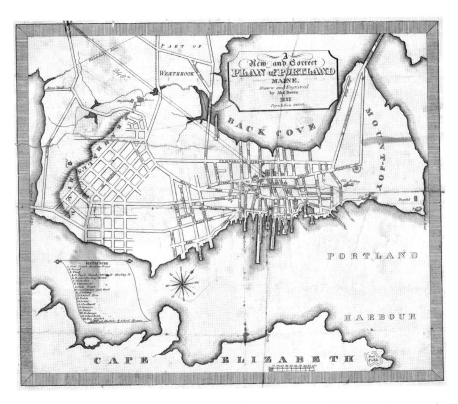

Drawn and engraved by Abel Bowen, this map shows street names, buildings, wharves and ropewalks of Portland, 1823. *Courtesy of the Collections of Maine Historical Society.*

famine of the 1830s forced many Irishmen to leave their country as a matter of survival, and they headed for America and Portland in numbers that greatly exceeded those of immigrants from other parts of the world. By 1860, they made up 11 percent of the city's total population.

In February 1823, Henry returned to Bowdoin College. After a six-hour stage ride, he remarked in a letter how very pleasant the ride was but also how he longed for spring and warmer days, as he enjoyed long walks in the woods: "I am only waiting for spring when we shall have warmer days—and more leisure, to enjoy myself." Henry was quite sick at times during his college years, remarking that he felt his best when on a pudding and milk diet, and he requested to his sisters to bake an oven full of molasses gingerbread. In a letter to his mother from Bowdoin College on March 1, 1823, he wrote, "I begin to think my health is some better than when I last wrote. As to pills—I would take them if you will send them to me but I do not want to taste any more of Brunswick medicine; I have had quite enough of that already."

Henry Wadsworth Longfellow's Peucinian Society medal, 1822. *Courtesy of the Collections of Maine Historical Society.*

On March 4, 1823, father Stephen was elected to the Eighteenth Congress as an Adams-Clay federalist. Serving from March 4, 1823, to March 3, 1825, he spent a considerable amount of time in Washington.

In March 1823, Henry Wadsworth Longfellow joined Bowdoin College's Peucinian Society, established in 1805 by eight students and originally called the Philomathian Society. The Peucinian Society's motto was *Pinos loquentes semper habemus* ("We always have the whispering pines"). A brief ceremony was held by Calvin E. Stowe, the secretary, who greeted candidates Henry Wadsworth Longfellow and Alfred Mason. With a pine branch extended in hand, Stowe said, "This we present you as a symbol of the society and emblematic of our connection. As we now unite our hands in the branches of the bough, may our hearts be united in affections and our endeavors in literary pursuits."

Henry again wrote to his father about his health: "I write to state my situation to you, and let you know how affairs stand. I am afraid that my health is declining, and I have good reason to think that my suspicions are not without foundation. I am somewhat troubled with an unpleasant feeling in my head." Stephen replied to his son telling him to guard his health, as "the greatest of temporal blessings prescribing a two mile walk daily and it's to be increased to four miles when better weather returns." Henry also wrote complaining that he was not receiving enough letters from family and asking for the *Portland Gazette* and the *Portland Argus*. He stated in a letter to his sister

Henry Wadsworth Longfellow's Bowdoin College tuition bill for the term ending January 1823. *Courtesy of the Collections of Maine Historical Society.*

Elizabeth "Betsey" that even "Old News [was] quite agreeable here." The *Portland Gazette* is the newspaper in which Henry's first published poem, "The Battle of Lovwell's Pond," appeared on November 17, 1820.

To his father, he said, "Why, in the name of Goodness, does not somebody write!" He noted that he had only received two letters from the family for the whole term, while he had written six. "I have not received the Papers, yet."

Trouble on the campus of Bowdoin College erupted when a student became ill in a church service at the Brunswick Congregational Church that the students were required to attend. Henry wrote:

> *We have had a famous scrape here a few days past. The whole town is literally up in arms. As the ill student, William Browne, left the service it was, noticed by Rev. Asa Mead. That afternoon Rev. Mead made remarks concerning the general behavior of the students, touching off a firestorm*

between the students and school government. A petition was drawn up by the students requesting to leave Rev. Mead and the Brunswick Congregational Church and to attend another service with a different preacher. A violent demonstration broke out after the faculty refused to let William Browne graduate with his class for his misbehavior.

Henry would later write to his father further on the instance:

All has become quiet again. Yet, Mr Mead seems not to have entirely got over his tantrams. He gave the students a few back-handers the last time he preached—talking a good deal about "deeds of darkness" to be brought to light here-after and so on. A few of the students have left his meeting: And I, also, want you to permit me to attend Parson Titcomb's. But I can spend no more time upon a subject so perfectly disgusting to me.

Stephen Longfellow replied on April 12, 1823: "Mr Mead may have been indiscreet, the action of the students in scraping him was most improper. I most sincerely Hope, that my sons have had nothing to do with this unfortunate and disgraceful transaction." No mention was made of Henry's request to attend a different church service.

Poet Thomas Gray was born in Cornhill, London, England, in 1716. He started writing poetry in 1742 after the death of his close friend Richard West. While at Bowdoin College, Henry would discover Gray's works, writing to his mother:

I have this evening been reading a few pages in Gray's Odes. I am very much pleased with them. The Progress of Poesy and the ode To Eton College are admirable. And many passages in The Bard, tho' I confess, quite obscure to me, seem to partake in a great degree of the sublime. Obscurity is the great objection which many urge against Gray. They do not consider that it contributes in the highest degree to sublimity. And he certainly aim'd at sublimity in these Lyrical Odes. If he did not so much the more honor to him, for he has certainly attained it, whether sought or unsought. Tho' not in themselves entirely original, they were quite so to me—and of course very amusing.

From the Thomas Gray poem "The Progress of Poesy" comes the following: "The Laughing flowers that round them blow. Drink life and fragrance as they flow. Now the rich stream of music winds along. Deep, majestic, smooth, and strong."

His mother replied:

> *I am not very conversant with the poetry of Gray, dear Henry, therefore I
> cannot tell whether I should be as much pleased with it, in general, as you are.
> His Elegy I have read frequently, and always with pleasure. I admire it for
> its truth and simplicity, and think it charming thing. I presume you will not
> allow it any sublimity. Obscurity is favorable to the sublime, you think. It may
> be so, but I am much better pleased with those pieces that touch the feelings and
> improve the heart than those that excite the imagination only and raise perhaps
> an indistinct admiration. That is an admiration of we know not exactly what.*

Henry continued to defend Thomas Gray's work, writing again to his
mother, "The partial and uncandid manner in which Dr Johnson, criticized
the poems of Gray, gives great offense to many, and is condemned by all of
candid minds. The causes of his severities are generally believed to be the
difference of their religious and political opinions." Zilpah replied, "I do
not think the Dr. possessed much sensibility for the charms of poetry, and
he was sometimes most unmerciful in his criticisms." Samuel Johnson (here
referred to as "Dr. Johnson"), an English writer and the author of *The Lives
of the Poets*, had written of Gray, "He published The Progress of Posey and
The Bard, two compositions at which readers of poetry were at first content
to gaze in mute amazement. Some that tried them confessed their inability
to understand them."

On May 11, 1823, Henry wrote to his mother about the ending of the
term for that year and again spoke of Thomas Gray: "I do not think it will
be in my power to bring you Gray's Poems. The volume which I had was
from the College Library. However I think I can get it for you in Portland."

In July 1823, the first steamboat arrived at Portland Harbor—the first
ever brought to Maine, in fact. It was the *Patent*, owned by Captain Seward
Porter of Portland, who had purchased the ship in New York for the use as a
passenger boat between Portland and Boston.

Henry spent time in Portland and in Gorham before returning to Bowdoin
College on October 3, 1823: "We have just got settled in our new room. It
is a very pleasant corner room in the third story of the North End of the
new building." During this term, Henry was reading three to four books at
a time. Mentioned are C.B. Brown's *Arthur Mervyn* and William Wirt's *The
Letters of the British Spy*.

In a letter to his sister Anne on October 26, 1823, Henry wrote about his
latest school assignment:

Last Friday the appointments for the December Exhibitions were given out. The part assigned me to perform, is a dialogue with JW. Bradbury. Or as it was given out by the president, "English Dialogue between a North American savage and an English Emigrant." We have 4 minutes a-piece: and the part is a high one, being the third in this division of the class. I think it be a very fine subject both to write and speak apon, and although it is not the part I wished for, yet I have this consolation that it is much higher than that, which I expected, so that I have every reason to be satisfied and well pleased with this appointment.

Longfellow was to play King Philip and Bradbury, Miles Standish. The exhibition would take place in December.

Bowdoin classmate Daniel Haraden Griffin died on November 8, 1823, at the age of twenty-three. Henry wrote to his mother on his classmate's death, "One of our best classmates died on Friday night or rather on Saturday morning last, after a short sickness of about 3 weeks, and all things are pretty gloomy here at present. He was one of the most mild and kindhearted students in College, bearing a character of the strictest morality. His complaints were consumptive and his loss is greatly felt amongst us. The class will attend his funeral at Freeport, tomorrow."

Stephen and Henry would return home for Thanksgiving break only to return to Bowdoin in late November. In December, Henry wrote to his father and sister Elizabeth about the exhibition in which he had performed as part of the Bowdoin college assignment. He told his father:

The Exhibition took place last evening and I must confess I feel glad it is past. The weather was very unpleasant yesterday. There was during the day quite a violent snow storm, and the evening was cold and uncomfortable. The audience of course was not very numerous, though the seats were better filled than I expected, considering the state of the weather. I feel a great weight is removed from my shoulders, for I could not but feel some solicitude, though I would never confess it. I shall now have a great deal more leisure, which to me is one of the sweetest things in the world.

To Elizabeth, Henry wrote not only of the exhibition at Bowdoin but also some amusing and stern lines regarding his dissatisfaction with the family not writing to him:

I am at a loss how to account for your long silence, and know not what to attribute it to, unless it be indisposition or a want of inclination, for I cannot but think you have time enough. To indisposition I am unwilling to attribute it, besides had you been so much out of health as to be unable to write. I should have heard of it from some other of the family. Upon your want of inclination the reason of your long silence must devolve. And here a heavy charge lies at your door, to which you must either immediately plead guilty or assert your innocence in a special manner. The only letter I find as coming from you, was written during the second week of this term and bears the date of October 8th. You see by this how negligent you are, it being more than two months since your last letter was received. For my own part I cannot imagine how you are going to excuse yourself and I shall not excuse you unless you write immediately upon the reception of this letter, or at farthest before the end of this week. It is now three weeks since I passed Thank{s}giving-day at home with you, and not a solitary mark or token of recollection from any one of you at home excepting one letter from mother. I do not see how you can be pardoned unless you turn over a new leaf. After a long process of time the Exhibition is at length over, and I have regained my liberty again—that is my leisure. The performance took place on Wednesday Evening last. During the day we had a considerable snow-storm; if snow fell with you at Portland, you will know exactly what an evening it was for a publick Exhibition. However the evening came—and the Exhibition too—but as for the audience—we will not say much about it. The female part was great—say for instance two ladies, which considering the unpleasant state of the weather was in fact as many as I expected. The Chapel was however apparently full, but whether students or town's-people I know and care not. I was glad there were but few ladies present, for my part was notsuch as would have pleased them, since it was so un-poetical, (as a dialog must be,) as not to please myself. Not that ladies are always fond of poetry, but an Indian Dialogue. Oh! dear! I was very much chagrined at having such an appointment. There is no doubt but that it ranked as high as it should have ranked, but I always disliked any such part at an Exhibition and was very desirous of having something else instead thereof, whenever I should come upon the stage. But it is now of no great consequence, since it is all over. I presume it will be something different when I have another appointment. If it is not I shall be terribly nervous. And now I will you another piece of NEWS. Your friend W.H. Codman delivered a Poem before the Athenean Society. I dare say it is something new to you that he was a poet. I have known this for a year or two, but I never dreamt that the little man would mount into the pulpit to deliver a poem. I can hardly give you a description of it until I come home. It was not at all original and yet it was quite interesting and quite as good as could have been expected, taking all things into consideration. We had a little more snow this evening and I presume we shall have excellent sleighing for a few weeks at least. I have had one sleigh-ride already and that is begin{n}ing remarkably early for me. I rather think you folks at home cannot amuse yourselves much in that way present. However when I return I mean to exercise the colt, pretty often. I have written twice to Washington, but as yet get no answers. I suppose it is hardly time to talk about them yet, though I presume you have heard from thence, before this date. And now I shall conclude my letter by strictly charging you, under the severe penalty of my royal displeasure, to write me straightway a long letter full of news, great and small, and now you may give my love to all, and I will make my best bow and retire from your presence. Your affectionate brother, H.W. Longfellow. Ps. The term ends on the 10th of Jany.

Henry spent Christmas Day at Bowdoin College writing to his mother and brother Alexander, while also spending part of the day reading from Washington Irving's *The Sketch Book*, from the fifth number consisting of "Christmas," "The Stage Coach," "Christmas Eve" and "Christmas Day." Longfellow was a fan of Irving's and *The Sketch Book*, writing many years later of his first experience with the book, "I was a school-boy when it was published, and read each succeeding number with ever increasing wonder and delight, spellbound by its pleasant humor, its melancholy tenderness, its atmosphere of revery,—nay, even by its gray-brown covers, the shaded letters of its titles, and the fair clean type."

The school term ended in January, and Henry's plan was to go to Boston with his friend and classmate Eugene Weld, who was originally from that city and had recently moved to Brunswick with his family. But father Stephen had different plans for his son's trip: Henry would go to Boston on the stage along with his Aunt Lucia. His aunt would leave the stage in Salem, and Henry would eventually meet up with his friends in Boston. He later wrote of his trip to his father, "I had a delightful visit. We went to Charlestown,—to the Navy yard and Breed's hill,—to the Athaneaum, to the State House, and took a beautiful view from the dome,—To Stewart's painting room, to Dogget's Repository,—and to all places of repute excepting the Mill-dam."

Henry returned to Bowdoin College from his trip and continue to work hard at his studies, although his brother Stephen did not. The record shows that Stephen was suspended by the Bowdoin authorities for neglect of duties, for participating in conduct "disturbing to the quietness and dishonorable to the character of a literary institution" and for introducing spirituous liquors into the college. This information came from the Bowdoin Faculty Records archive, dated December 28, 1824. In March of that year, Henry wrote of his brother's conduct to their mother:

> *His conduct seems to be pretty much as it was last term. He is absent from his room most of the time, and I do not know how much he studies, although he does not appear very well at recitation. I am now sorry I have told, what I have told. It is too near the beginning of the term to judge of what he will do. Excepting this apparent negligence, his conduct is perfectly regular. You see in what a very unpleasant situation you have placed me, by setting me as a spy upon him. If I do not tell you the truth of the matter, I shall not be doing my duty, and yet when I tell you the truth, I am afraid you will interpret things worse than they really are. Don't write papa about it for I am certain he will be more apt to do so than you are. I cannot say anymore.*

Stephen Longfellow was in Washington at the time and wrote to his son of his poor conduct. In May 1824, Henry was vaccinated by Dr. Wells for smallpox at Bowdoin. The city of Portland did not experience a widespread outbreak of the disease, and on April 27, 1824, both the *Eastern Argus* and the *Portland Gazette* reported on the disease. The *Argus* noted, "We understand that no new case of Small Pox has occurred since the 21st, and it is believed that the measures adopted to prevent the disorder from spreading, have been perfectly successful." The *Gazette* reported, "Small Pox: We continue to publish statements of the Selectmen and the Physicians concerning the extent to which this disease exists in this town; and as we shall strictly adhere to our determination to give the facts without any colouring or diminution, and from authority which must be conclusive, we trust that no unnecessary alarm will be excited by groundless or exaggerated reports, when the whole truth will be laid fairly before the public from facts, not surmises."

On May 3, 1824, a town meeting was held, and Portland residents voted to form a committee to determine a plan, a place and the expense for a building that could house a hospital. The chair of that committee was Lemuel Moody, who had built the Portland Observatory in 1807. The hospital was called City Hospital on Mountjoys Neck, now "Munjoy Hill."

On September 25, 1824, a poem was published in the *Portland Advertiser* written by the seventeen-year-old Henry. It was written in protest of the removal of the wooden church known as "Old Jerusalem," where the Longfellow family attended church services:

Our fathers' temple! O'er thy form
In peace time's holy twilight falls;
Yet heavenly light glows pure and warm
The shades of years have mellow'd long
But not obscur'd that light of God
Though they that plac'd thee here shall throng
No more the courts where once they trod.

The Longfellow children would bring a foot warmer to the old church because it was so cold and the sermons so long. In a bit of Longfellow folklore, the new church was built in 1825, and to this day there exists one of the family's foot warmers in the Longfellow pew.

Henry returned to Bowdoin after a brief holiday in Portland to complete his term. On October 29, 1824, Henry delivered a "Salutatory Oration in Latin" called *Angli Poetae* ("English Poets") as the first event of the program celebrating the resumption of the term. Nathaniel Hawthorne would appear in the eighth spot of the program, offering his Latin dissertation *De Patribus Conscriptis Romanorum* ("Of Roman Senators"). Born Nathaniel Hathorne on July 4, 1804, in Salem, Massachusetts, to Nathaniel Hathorne and the former Elisabeth Clarke Manning, he was the great-grandson of Judge John Hathorne, a man involved with the Salem witch trials. Nathaniel would later add the *w* to make "Hawthorne" in order to hide his relation to his great-grandfather.

Hawthorne entered Bowdoin College in 1821. On the way to the college, the stage would stop in Portland, Maine, where Nathaniel Hawthorne met Franklin Pierce. They became friends, and in later years, Hawthorne wrote a biography of the former president. In 1816, Hawthorne's family moved to Maine, and for three years, Hawthorne lived in Raymond, Maine, close to Sebago Lake. He recalled his time in Maine, "Those were delightful days, for that part of the country was wild then, with only scattered clearings, and nine tenths of it primeval woods."

Hawthorne was elected to Phi Beta Kappa in 1824 and graduated from Bowdoin College in the class of 1825 along with classmate Henry Wadsworth Longfellow. Years later, Hawthorne described his college years to Richard Henry Stoddard: "I was educated (as the phrase is) at Bowdoin College, I was an idle student, negligent of college rules and the Procrustean details of academic life, rather choosing to nurse my own fancies than to dig into Greek roots and be numbered among the learned Thebans." He went on to have his novels and short stories published, such as *The Scarlet Letter* in 1850 and *The House of the Seven Gables* in 1852.

In November 1824, Henry wrote to George Wadsworth Wells and, in December, to his father, Stephen. In both of these letters, his concern was about his future. To Wells he wrote, "Somehow, and yet I hardly know why, I am unwilling to study any profession. I cannot make a lawyer of any eminence, because I have not a talent for argument; I am not good enough for a minister,—and as to Physic, I utterly and absolutely detest it."

To his father, he wrote:

> I take this early opportunity to write you, because I wish to know fully your inclination with regard to the profession I am to pursue, when I leave college. For my part, I have already hinted to you what would best please me. I want to spend one year at Cambridge for the purpose of reading History, and of becoming familiar with the best authors in polite literature: whilst at the same time I can be acquiring a knowledge of the Italian Language, without an acquaintance with which, I shall be shut out from one of the most beautiful departments of letters. The French I mean to understand pretty thoroughly before I leave College. After leaving Cambridge I would attach myself to some literary periodical publication, by which I could maintain and still enjoy the advantages of reading. Now I do not think there is anything visionary and chimerical in my plan thus far. The fact is—and I will disguise it in the least, for I think I ought not,—the fact is, I most eagerly aspire after future eminence in literature, my whole soul burns most ardently for it, and every earthly thought centers in it. There may be something visionary in this, but I flatter myself, that I have prudence enough to keep my enthusiasm from defeating its own object by too great haste. Surely there never was a better opportunity offered for the exertion of literary talent in our country, than is now offered. To be sure, most of our literary men, thus far, have not been professedly so, until they have studied and entered the practice of Theology, Law, or Medicine. But this is evidently lost time. I do believe that we ought to pay more attention to the opinion of Philosophers, that nothing but nature can qualify a man for knowledge. Whether Nature has given me any capacity for knowledge or not, she has at any rate given me a very strong predilection for literary pursuits, and I am almost confident in believing, that if I can ever rise in the world, it must be by the exercise of my talents in the wide field of literature. With such a belief I must say, that I am unwilling to engage in the study of the Law. Had I an inclination to become an orator, not this inclination, nor any application to the study of oratory, could constitute me one, unless Nature had given me a genius for that pursuit. This I think will hold good in it's

application to all the professions of life, and of course to literary pursuits. Here, than, seems to be the starting point; and I think it best for me to float out into the world upon that tide, and in that channel, which will soonest bring me to my destined port;—and not to struggle against both wind and tide, and by attempting what is impossible, lose everything.

In December 1824, Stephen Longfellow wrote to his son, "Epistolary composition is one of the most difficult kind[s] of style to acquire, and is at the same time a most desirable attainment; and if you mean to become iminent as a literary man you must remember that taste and scholarship are as much displayed in correspondence as in any excircise."

Longfellow had three of his poems published in the *United States Literary Gazette* during 1824: "Thanksgiving," "Autumnal Nightfall" and "Italian Scenery." On February 1, 1825, "Woods in Winter" was published in the *Gazette*:

"WOODS IN WINTER"

When winter winds are piercing chill,
   And through the hawthorn blows the gale,
With solemn feet I tread the hill,
   That over-brows the lonely vale.

O'er the bare upland, and away
   Through the long reach of desert woods,
The embracing sunbeams chastely play,
   And gladden their deep solitudes.

Where twisted round the barren oak
   The summer vine in beauty clung,
And summer winds the stillness broke,
   The crystal icicle is hung.

Where from their frozen urns mute springs
   Pour out the river's gradual tide,
Shrilly the skater's iron rings,
   And voices fill the woodland side.

Alas! how changed from the fair scene
   When birds sang out their mellow lay

And winds were soft, and woods were green,
*   And the song ceased not the day!*

But still wild music is abroad,
*   Pale, desert wood! within your crowd;*
And gathering winds, in hoarse accord,
*   Amid the vocal reeds pipe loud.*

Chill airs and wintry winds! my ear
*   Has grown familiar with your song;*
I hear it in the opening year,
*   I listen, and it cheers me long.*

Stephen would return to Portland after his term in the U.S. Congress expired in 1825. That year, Portland would receive a most exciting visitor in the form of Revolutionary War hero the Marquis de Lafayette:

Town meeting notice, Portland, 1825. *Courtesy of the Collections of Maine Historical Society.*

"Sprague's Journal of Maine History"
The Old Maine Historical and Genealogical Recorder
(Vol. 4, no. 4)
General LaFayette Visit to Portland, Maine

About 9 o'clock A.M. (June 24, 1825), General LaFayette entered the town of Portland.

Although he had been the round of the whole country, and received the attentions and gratulations of a whole nation for almost a year, so that the subject might be supposed in some degree to have lost it's novelty, yet we doubt whether he had in any place met with a more cordial and warm reception than in this town; and what is more remarkable, notwithstanding the whole year of fatigue duty which he had gone through, witnessing almost the same scenes from day to day, yet he showed not the least mark of apathy, but seemed to greet the old war-worn veterans of the Revolution with as much enthusiasm, to exchange salutations with the public functionaries with much animation, and to shake hands with thousands who thronged around him with as much feeling and affection as he possibly could have done on his first arrival in this country. On his arrival in Portland, he was met by the Committee of Arrangements, the Selectmen. And citizens of the town on Bramhall's hill, where he was addressed by the Hon. Stephen Longfellow in behalf of the citizens, to which the General replied as usual. A procession was formed to escort him through the towns, including his son and Mons LaVasseur. The military escort consisted of four companies of light troops. They were the Portland light infantry, the Rifle Company, Mechanic blues and Brunswick light Infantry; the latter with a sprit that did them much credit, voluntarily marched from Brunswick to this place, a distance, of twenty-six miles, in complete uniform, to join the escort of the day. About fifty truck men dressed in white frocks appeared in the cavalcade and added much to the appearance of the procession. The General rode in an open carriage, drawn by four white horses, his head uncovered and accompanied by Colonel Dunlap. The procession, as it moved through the principal streets of the town, passed under many beautiful arches of evergreen and roses thrown across the streets in different localities; one across Danforth street, at the intersection of High, with the inscription, "WELCOME LAFAYETTE," "BRANDYWINE 1777," another across the head of Free street, on which a live eagle was perched, at-id on the arch these inscriptions—"WASHINGTON AND LAFAYETTE," "WELCOME CHEVALIER," "SANS PRUR ET SANS REP.—ROACH." On Free street the school children numbering about twelve hundred all dressed in uniform greeted him; the girls holding wreaths of flowers which they waved at the general and threw into the street as he passed; and the boys wore badges—of blue ribbon on their hats inscribed with "WELCOME LAFAYETTE." The General looked on them, with affectionate interest as he passed with his head uncovered before them. An arch was erected at the foot of Free street, inscribed with "WELCOME TO OUR PARRIS." Across Middle at the head of Exchange street, was an arch inscribed "YORKTOWN." At the head of King street another, on which stood a FULL RIGGED MINIATURE SHIP, and upon the arch was inscribed "I SHALL PURCHASE AND FIT OUT A VESSEL FOR—MYSELF." Another arch was thrown across Congress street in front of the Universalist church and near the State House, where the Governor and Council were waiting. Salutes were fired on Bramhall's Hill, Mount Joy and Fort Preble; and the bells rung during the movement of the procession. It was estimated that near fifteen thousand people saw LaFayette—during the few hours he remained in the town. A platform was erected in front—of the State House and covered with an extensive awning where the General was addressed by President Allen of Bowdoin College and in presence of the officers and students of the college, received the honorary degree of Doctor of Laws. After some time spent in greetings, the procession moved to the house of Daniel Cobb on Free street, where lodgings had been prepared for the General. Here refreshments were taken, and here also was addressed in behalf of the Grand lodge of Maine, by William Swan, Grand Master, and other members of the Fraternity. And as LaFayette could not extend his journey beyond Portland, he was addressed here by the citizens of Thomaston, Bath, Hallowell, Augusta and Gardiner; to all of which the General responded in his happy way. At 4 o'clock the General partook of a public dinner at Union Hall, which was prepared and served in elegant style. The guest spent the evening at the house—of Governor Parris, which was thrown open to the citizens. Lafayette left town Sunday morning about 7 o'clock without any parade and returned to Saco on his way to Vermont. He took breakfast at Captain Spring's in Biddeford, tarried a short time with Colonel Emery, and attended divine service at the church of Rev. Mr. Tracy; immediately after which, he set out for Concord where he arrived the same night.

Colonel Caleb Emery and Captain Seth Spring were both veterans of the Revolutionary War.

Records show that Lafayette arrived in Portland on June 24, 1825. Longfellow sent this poem to Nathaniel Low, editor of the *American Patriot*, a Portland newspaper, on June 25, 1825, from Bowdoin College. Apparently, he had written the poem prior to Lafayette's visit to Portland. The poem appeared in the *American Patriot* on July 1, 1825:

"LaFayette"

Here Shall the Hero rest:
 True hearts are round him!
Those he has nobly bless'd,
 Nobly have crown'd him
Many a tongue hath said
 God speed the Stranger!—
Many a heart, that bled,
 Owns its avenger.—

Ne'er shall our Eagle stoop,
 Crest-fall'n and daunted!—
Ne'er shall the banner droop
 Strong hands have planted!—
Those that in days of grief
 Conquer'd beneath it,
Now with the Olive leaf
 Hasten to wreath it.

Europe has seen from far
 Mid her thick legions,
Empire's fast-westering star
 Shine on these regions.—
Why does she wear the yoke,
 And free hearts falter?—

Why is the quench'd urn broke
 At Freedom's alter?—

Father!—we bring thee
 Fervent—devotion;
It bursts from hearts as free

As the free Ocean!—
Here in our bosoms rest;
   True hearts are round thee!
Those thou hast nobly bless'd
   Nobly have crown'd thee!—

Pulci.—

His reason for using the signature "Pulci" is enigmatic; Luigi Pulci, a fifteenth-century Italian poet, was the "sire of half-serious rhyme [Byron]," as noted in *The Letters of Henry Wadsworth Longfellow*. One month after Lafayette's visit, Henry's grandmother Elizabeth Wadsworth passed away.

Appointments for commencement were given out, and Henry was to present third; he was to graduate fourth in Bowdoin's class of 1825. Writing to his sister Anne, he noted:

My appointment, they tell me, is considered the fourth in the class—having only Little, Dean and Bradbury above me. How I came to get so high, is rather a mistery to me, in as much as I have never been a remarkably hard student, touching College studies, except during my Sophomore year, when I used to think that I was studying pretty hard—though I might possibly have been mistaken. In five weeks we shall be set free from college—for one month. Then comes Commencement—and than—and than—I cannot say what will be, after that.

Classmate Gorham Dean, who was to present third in the commencement, died of consumption on August 11, 1825, just a few weeks before the celebration was to take place. Dean had been assigned a "Philosophical Disquisition."

The graduating class of 1825 would be the largest for Bowdoin College, and commencement was the most important day for students and faculty. A host of Maine's elite also gathered to watch the graduation.

From the wooden platform, Longfellow read his commencement oration:

To an American there is something endearing in the very sound's—Our Native Writers. Like the music of our native tongue, when heard in a foreign land, they have power to kindle up within him the tender memory of his home and fireside;—and more than this, they foretell that whatever is noble and attractive in our national character will one day be associated

Image of Bowdoin College's campus in 1862. *Courtesy of the Collections of Maine Historical Society.*

with sweet magic of Poetry. Is then our land to be indeed the land of song? Will it one day be rich in romantic associations? Will poetry, that hallows every scene,—that renders every spot classical,—and pours out on all things the soul of its enthusiasm, breath over it that enchantment, which lives in the isles of Greece, and is more than life amid the woods, that wave o'er Delphi's steep? Yes—and palms are to be won by our native writers!—by those, that have been nursed and brought up with us in the civil and religious freedom of our country. Already has a voice been lifted up in this land,— already a spirit and a love of literature are springing up in the shadow of our free political institutions…

Of the many causes which have hitherto retarded the growth of polite literature in our country, I have not time to say much. The greatest, which now exists, is doubtless the want of that exclusive attention, which eminence in any profession so imperiously demands. Ours is an age and a country of great minds, though perhaps not of great endeavors. Poetry with us has never yet been anything but a pastime. The fault however is not so much that of our writers, as of prevalent modes of thinking which characterize our country and our times. We are a plain people, that have nothing to do with the mere pleasures and luxuries of life: and hence there has sprung up within us a quick-sightedness to the failings of literary men, and an aversion to everything that is not practical, operative, and thorough-going. But if we ever have a national literature, our native writers must be patronized. Whatever there may be in letters, over which time shall have no power, must be "born of great endeavors," and those endeavors are the offspring of liberal patronage. Putting off, then, what Shakespeare calls "the visage of the times,"—we must become hearty well-wishers to our native authors:— and with them there must be a deep and thorough conviction of the glory of their calling,—an utter abandonment of everything else,—and a noble self-devotion to the cause of literature. We have indeed much to hope from these things:—for our hearts are already growing warm towards literary adventurers, and a generous spirit has gone abroad in our land, which shall liberalize and enlighten…

Our poetry is not in books alone. It is in the hearts of those men, whose love for the world's gain,—for its business and its holiday, has grown cold within them, and who have gone into the retirements of nature, and have found there sweet sentiment, and pure devotion of feeling can spring up and live in the shadow of a low and quiet life, and amid those, that have no splendor in their joys, and no parade in their griefs.

There shall the mind take color from things around us:—from them shall there be a genuine birth of enthusiasm,—a rich development of the poetic feeling that shall break forth in song. Though the works of art must grow old and perish away from earth, the forms of nature shall keep forever their power over human mind, and have their influence upon the literature of a people.

Henry Wadsworth Longfellow's Phi Beta Kappa key, 1825. *Courtesy of the Collections of Maine Historical Society.*

Silhouettes of the famous class of 1825, Bowdoin College. *First row, left to right*: Nathaniel Hawthorne, John S.C. Abbott, George W. Pierce, Elisha Bacon, Richmond Bradford, Jeremiah Drummer and Cyrus Hamlin Coolidge. *Second row, left to right*: Henry Wadsworth Longfellow, Patrick Henry Greenleaf, Jonathan Cilley, Alden Boynton, Frederic Mellen, Samuel Page Benson and Mark Haskell Newman. *Third row, left to right*: David Shepley, William Hale, David Haley Foster, Alfred Martin, Nathaniel Dunn, Saward Wymand and Gorham Dean. *Fourth row, left to right*: Horatio Bridge, Thomas Ayer, Edward Joseph Vose, Charles Snell, Eugene Weld, John Dafforne Kinsman and George Barrell Cheever. *Fifth row, left to right*: Joseph Jenkins Eveieth, Joseph Stover Little, Hezekiah Packard, Alfred Mason, Charles Jeffrey Abbott, Stephen Longfellow and James Ware Bradbury. *Sixth row, left to right*: Edward Deering Preble, William Stone and Cullen Sawtelle. *Courtesy of the Collections of Maine Historical Society.*

We may rejoice, then, in the hope of beauty and sublimity in our national literature, for no people are richer than we are in the treasures of nature. And well may each of us feel a glorious and high-minded pride in saying, as he looks on the hills and vales,—on the woods and waters of New England,—"this is my own, my native land."

THE POET'S LETTERS AND LANGUAGES

At the commencement, Bowdoin College's governing body voted to establish a chair of modern languages. Henry Wadsworth Longfellow, just eighteen at the time, was recommended by the trustees and offered the position. For preparation for the new position, it was suggested by the trustees that he should study in Europe. This would be at his own expense for a period of two years. Stephen Longfellow broke the news to his son at their Portland home. Before Henry would leave for Europe, Stephen Longfellow would have his sons study law with three other boys: George Washington Pierce, Frederic Mellen and Patrick Greenleaf. They would refer to themselves as the "Knights of the Temple Bar." The knights would go on to write fourteen mainly satirical essays, which were published locally and without fanfare; the disappointed Temple Bar soon disbanded. As the boys studied law at the Longfellow home, the city of Portland continued to grow, along with its busy harbor.

The building that became city hall was built in Market Square in 1825 and was originally used as a military hall, becoming city hall in 1832, the year Portland became a city. The building over the years had many different uses and was known by a number of names: the Old City Hall, Old Town Hall and Old Market House. Market Square was very close to the Longfellow home.

In preparation for his trip abroad, Henry contacted the Honorable Charles Daveis, who studied law in Boston and would give Henry letters of introduction to his influential friends in that city. Henry had also called on others for letters of introduction. In late April 1926, he left Portland for Europe, first stopping in Boston. In a letter he wrote to his mother on May 2, 1926, he noted, "I dined

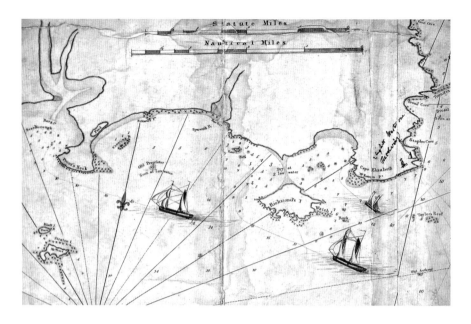

Above: Detail from *Map of Portland Harbor and Islands* by Lemuel Moody, 1825. *Courtesy of the Collections of Maine Historical Society.*

Left: Silhouette portrait of Henry Wadsworth Longfellow, 1825. *Courtesy of the Collections of Maine Historical Society.*

to day with Mr. Tinknor. He is a little Spanish-looking man, but exceedingly kind and affable. He has supplied me with letters to Washington Irving—Prof. Eichorn in Germany—and Robert Southey. He strongly recommends a year residence in Germany—and is very decidedly and strongly in favor of commencing literary studies there."

George Ticknor was professor of modern languages at Harvard. Johan Gottfried Eichhorn was Ticknor's professor at Gottingen and a friend. Henry continued:

One of Dr. Well's letters introduced me to Dr. Lowell who has given me a letter to the celebrated Mrs. Grant of Laggan—author of a poem, which you will find somewhere about the house, called the "Highlanders." Rev. Charles Lowell, West Unitarian church of Boston's pastor. Mrs. Anne McVickar Grant of Laggan, translator of Highland poetry and author of Memoirs of an American Lady (1808). On Monday I was at Cambridge and saw Pres. Kirkland. He is a jolly little man—and does not pretend to put on all that dignity and high decorum, which sometimes hang—and oddly enough, too, upon the shoulders of men in office. [John Thornton Kirkland was Harvard College president from 1810 to 1827.]

The second stop was the village of Northampton:

With the village of Northampton I was highly delighted. The mountain and river scenery near it are certainly very beautiful, and from Round Hill—the seat of Messrs Coggswell and Bancroft's school—you have an extensive view of the village and its environs. These gentlemen received me with the greatest kindness—and have furnished me with a number of excellent letters. They coincide with Prof. Ticknor of Cambridge in recommending a year's residence at Gottingen. Mr. Ticknor says that the expenses there will not be so great as at Paris, and that it is all-important to have a knowledge of the German language. The lectures on literary history, which he wishes me to attend there, commence in October, and he says I could before that time become sufficiently advanced [in] the language to understand them. I should take rooms there at Paris, and should pay about on guinea for a course of Lectures. It will, he thinks, be a solid foundation for future literary acquirements. For my own part—I must confess that this change in my original plan did not strike me very favorably at first—but the more I reflect upon it the better I like it. I wish you to write, at New York, as soon as you receive this—and tell me what you think of the change in my plans.

After reaching Albany, Henry wrote to his father:

> *Mr. Ticknor and Mr. Bancroft have both studied at Gottingen, and of course their opinion upon the subject is of much weight. At Northampton, I visited the Lead Mine, which lies about 8 miles from the village. They call it a Lead Mine by courtesy, because geologists say that a vein of lead ore runs somewhere in the vicinity and specimens have here and there been found. The entrance is at the side of a clay hill and the passage is roofed with timber—and is about 3 feet in height—measuring from the surface of water which everywhere fills the bottom of the cavern, and affords easy means of passage in and out by boat. You soon however reach the solid granite, thro' which an excavation has been made to the distance of nine hundred feet, making the length of the whole cavern about one thousand. The height of the cave, after it reaches the granite, varies from three to ten feet;—and the whole passage is made by the traveller in a little flat bottomed boat, in which he stretches himself upon his back and is propelled forward by a kind of ragged Palinurus, who navigates the boat by pushing his feet against the roof of the cavern, where it is low enough—and where it is not by means of a pole thrust against the rocky sides, which are on an average about 5 or 6 feet distant from each other. The whole business is very curious—and certainly the cave is a monument of human perseverance— since after more than twenty years labor no vein has been found. The Perkinses of Boston are the principal proprietors,—and the man who lives in the nearest cottage has worked the mine for eleven years.*

The third stop was Hudson:

> *I therefore stopped at Hudson, and went down by land to Red Hook, where I passed Sunday afternoon. The scenery on the North River between Albany and Hudson is very beautiful, especially where the river makes a gradual sweep round a low point of land, and you catch the last view of Albany. There is something very peculiar and singular in the style of buildings which one here sees in the little Dutch farm-houses—constructed partly of stone and partly of small Holland bricks—with thatch-roofed barns and out-houses. I sketched one or two of them on the back of a letter which will give you a faint idea of them.*

The following is from a letter to his sister Elizabeth after he arrived in New York City, written one day before he would leave New York for Europe:

Red Hook is a very beautiful little village—and from it you have a fine view of the blue peaks of the Catskill Mountains, stretching up to a noble height, and lording it over the surrounding country. On the afternoon of Sunday [May 7] I attended the village church. It is a small and simple building, standing upon a little eminence and surrounded by its church-yard. The villagers have a beautiful and romantic custom of placing a slender white railing around the graves of their friends, and of planting flowers within them. Some of the grave stones were over-run with moss, whilst others covered with the wild rose, with osiers bending over them. I left Red Hook on Monday, but did not reach this city till 4 o'clock on Tuesday morning [May 9]. I was exceedingly disappointed in not seeing The Highlands by daylight after all my delay for that purpose.

Stop number four was Albany, and Henry wrote to his father at length: "I have reached this dirty city:—this morning from Northampton. I shall not however remain here long enough to visit any public buildings." To sister Elizabeth, he also wrote of Albany: "[It] is certainly a very dirty place."

The fifth stop was New York. He wrote to sister Elizabeth, "I went to Philadelphia on Wednesday—remained there but on day and returned to this place on Friday." To sister Anne, he wrote:

I was in Brooklyn on Wednesday—the same day on which I arrived in this city. It was about sunset, and I found both Uncle and Aunt at home. I saw them again yesterday;—dined with them, and went to the Navy Yard with them—and am every moment expecting Uncle here. I have been very much delighted with Aunt Louisa—every way delighted with her—and yet I am very well aware, that I can give you no description of her person sufficiently correct to enable you to form any idea of her appearance. She is just about your own size, but her figure is entirely different from yours;—I know not whose it resembles—nor indeed do I know who has countenance resembling hers. Her complection is very dark—and her eyes black and brilliant—and whole face very expressive and very intellectual. By the way—I am going over tomorrow morning to take breakfast with her, and say good bye for the last time. I sail for Le Havre de Grace tomorrow at 10 o'clock, in the fore-noon, on board the Ship Cadmus, Capt. Allen. She left the wharf yesterday noon, and the passengers are to be taken down the bay to her by the Steam Boat Nautilus. There are twenty cabin passengers, two of which are ladies—and many of the gentlemen are French, which will be of great advantage to me. The ship is a very fine one and the Capt. has a reputation of being an excellent man. This will make everything as pleasant as can be; and at this season of the year I cannot but anticipate a good passage. I was not so much pleased with Philadelphia as I expected to be. It is not half so pleasant to me as New York. Whilst there I visited Pratt's Garden and the water Works at Fair Mount.

While Henry was in Philadelphia, he would meet with Captain John Derby; his wife, Eleanor Coffin Derby; and their daughter, Sarah Ellen Derby. They would all attend a sociable evening with dancing. Eleanor was the daughter of Dr. Nathanial Coffin of Portland, and they were friends with the Longfellow family. Henry also wrote in a letter to sister Anne, "Carey and Lea—the Philadelphia booksellers will publish the second volume of the Atlantic Souvenir in October next. I forgot to tell you that the pieces I wrote you were entitled 'The Spirit of Poetry'—'The Burial of the Minnisink'—'Song of the Birds'—and 'The Dead Bird'—a ballad."

The "Song of the Birds" (following) and "Burial of the Minnisink" appeared in *The Atlantic Souvenir: A Christmas and New Year's Offering* in 1827. "The Spirit of Poetry" would appear in the annual's next addition. What was not published was the poem Henry spoke of called "The Dead Bird."

"Song of the Birds"

With what a hollow dirge its voice did fill
The vast and empty hallow of the night!—
It had perched itself upon a tall old tree,
That hung its tufted and thick clustering leaves
Midway across the brook; and sung most sweetly,
In all the merry and heart-broken sadness
Of those that love hath crazed. Clearly it ran
Through all the delicate compass of its voice:—
And then again, as from a distant hollow,
I heard its sweet tones like an echo sounding,
And coming, like the memory of a friend
From a far distant country—or the silent land
Of the mourned and the dead, to which we all are passing;
It seemed the song of some poor broken heart,
Haunted forever with love's cruel fancies!—
Of one that has loved much yet never known
The luxury of being loved again!

But when the morning broke, and the green woods
Were all alive with birds—with what a clear
And ravishing sweetness sung the plaintive thrush;
I love to hear its delicate rich voice,
Chanting through all the gloomy day, when loud
Amid the trees is dropping the big rain,
And gray mists wrap the hills;—for aye the sweeter
Its song is, when the day is sad and dark. And thus,
When the bright fountains of a woman's love
Are gently running over, if a cloud
But darken, with its melancholy shadow,
The bright flowers round our way, her heart
Doth learn new sweetness, and her rich voice falls
With more delicious music on our ears.

On May 15, 1826, Henry boarded the ship *Cadmus* for Europe. He wrote first to his mother on June 15, 1826, from Havre de Grace, "I have at length reached the shores of the Old World. We arrived yesterday at four o'clock P.M. and I employ the first leisure moment to send you tidings of my safety."

The voyage took thirty days, and there were no storms to speak of, as Henry wrote in his first letter from Europe: "The sea was so smooth that the whole voyage might have been safely made in a yawl boat." Henry described Havre de Grace in the same letter:

The houses are all of stone or small yellow bricks—very narrow and most of them five—and many six stories high—with "peticoat and pantaloons" dangling from the upper windows, and linen hung out to dry on little balconies. The streets are most of them paved with flat stones about six inches square,—without side-walks—and sloping down from the buildings on each side to a little gutter in the middle, something in this manner. The fortifications of the city, which are now somewhat out of repair are very extensive. If my memory serves me they were commenced by Louis 13th—and finished by Louis 14th. The eastern part is defended by a double ditch forty feet in width with ramparts thirty of forty in height. Beyond these lies the most beautiful part of the city—the commercial part being very low, dingy and dirty. But east of the gates the land rises abruptly—sloping to the south east—covered with the richest verdure—with the country-houses of the citizens rising terrace above terrace to the very top. The antique

*buildings with peaked roofs and tall chimneys,—peeping out from amid
the trees have a very romantic and beautiful appearance.*

Henry's plan after arriving in Havre de Grace was to leave on a steamboat
for Rouen. His plans were drastically changed when his trunk was seized by
police, and he was forced to obtain a passport:

*You perceive in what great haste I write, I leave in a few minutes in the
Steam Boat for Rouen. I thought I should have written to Stephen and the
girls and all whilst at Havre—but I did not get my trunk from the Police
Office till 10 o'clock this morning—and my whole writing apparatus was
contained in them, which has prevented me from putting my good designs
into practice. But I know that you will be well satisfied to hear of my safe
arrival, and that I am in the best possible health. Our passage was so much
longer than all on board anticipated, that we have arrived barley in season
to send letters by the Queen Mab, which sails this evening.*

Henry also wrote to his brother Stephen that same day:

*Having lost my passage to Rouen by delay in obtaining a passport, I am
obliged to remain another night in this city:*

*And to complete the catastrophy, instead of journeying up the fair waters
of the Seine in the Steam boat as I intended, I shall be jolted and jostled
along a rough highway in a French diligence. I have been much pleased
with this city, because about it is perfectly novel to me. What first attracted
my attention, as we came solely up the quai, was the singular construction
of the houses, all of which are old and much dilapidated. No description
can give you any conception of their quaint and peculiar style—though you
can conceive how odd a spectacle it must be to see in a street of only one
rod's width, with tall dingy houses six stories high—a grand display from
every upper window of blankets and bed-clothes—old shirts and sheets—
flapping in the wind—not to mention, loose pantaloons and petticoat,
pendant on dyer's pole afloat. As I walked from the ship to the hotel I
was irresistably seized with drivers fits of laughter. At almost every step
I encountered gens-d'armed with fierce whiskers and curling beard[s]—
women with wooden shoes full of feet and straw—paper hats and tight
pantaloons—and the dames of Normandy with tall pyramidal caps of
muslin—reaching at least two feet above the head, and adorned with long
ear-lappets.*

A French "table d'hote" is well worth mentioning from its novelty to a stranger. The first dish of course is soup,—and next they will bring you a piece of meat—of what kind you choose—but no bigger than your two fingers—and then they change your plate and give you a piece of a different kind—but the same size—and so on for ten or a dozen dishes. After the meats are removed they bring on the vegetables—then fruit—then cake. It is very amusing to see a Frenchman tuck his napkin under his chin and fall to—and yesterday the very paragon of Paddy Carey was at table. He was a great burly faced dragoon—a Big Dragoon—about seven feet high with nothing French about him but his language and his uniform and as this "proper man" talked with the landlady, I could not help think of Widow Leary and "pat so sly ogle throws"—which put me to mind of Ned Preble. [Ned Preble was a childhood friend of both Henry and Stephen who attended Bowdoin College and graduated in the class of 1825.] *If Ned only knew the one hundredth part of the laughable things I have seen during one day's residence in Havre, he would lament long and loud that he had not come to France with me. The fortifications of this city are very grand. I cannot describe them to you because I know not military terms enough to make you comprehend me:—but they seem to me to be impregnable. Beyond the gates of these, on the eastern side, are the Boulevards of the city, and beyond these a thickly wooded hill with country houses. In this direction, too, the roads leads you thro' an avenue of trees to the Havre Light Houses. But it waxes late and I start tomorrow at six. Ergo—good night. Did Pa receive a letter from me concerning going to Germany? I put this in the form of a question tho' all I intend is to say that I wrote upon the subject—before I reached New York. You will of course remember me particularly to all my particular friends without my being more particular;—and as to the family, they all know how much love I bear them, without a repetition of the old saying about poor pens and pale ink—et cetera. I shall not write again before I reach Paris—when I shall open upon Fred—and Ned—and Pat—and all who are to be my correspondents. Fare-well. Your affectionate brother, Henry.* [Henry refers here to two other good friends besides Ned Preble: Frederick Mellen and Patrick Greenleaf, who were also graduates of Bowdoin College's class of 1825.]

Henry reached Paris on June 18, 1826, received by his second cousin Ebenezer Storer, who was studying medicine; Storer had reserved a room for Henry with Madame Potet and her two adopted daughters. She ran a boardinghouse where Henry and six other boarders would stay. "Madame P.," as Henry affectionately called her, referred to the gentleman boarders as "sons." Henry wrote to his father in a letter dated June 20:

I intend to reside here whilst I remain in Paris. You cannot conceive how very fortunate I am in getting into this family. Madame Potet is one of the best women in the world, and tho' I have been here but two days I feel myself perfectly at home. Madame P has two daughters with her, the elder of which is about twelve or thirteen years old—the other about eight. The younger is engaged to a gentleman twenty one years old, which may seem strange to all of you, tho' it is common custom in France to engage all little girls of about that age. The elder performs most elegantly on the Piano-forte, which adds much to our pleasures here;—since she plays with nearly as much ease and elegance as Nolcini himself. [Henry studied music with Nolcini in Portland.] *I know of but one objection to my residing here whilst at Paris, and that is that there are seven of us boarders— "Sons," as Madame calls us—all Americans. Perhaps you will think there is danger of speaking too much English—and there would be indeed, if we were much together—but we seldom assemble except at meals at which all English is forbidden—and he who speaks a word of it is fined one sou. Moreover three of the boarders have resided some time in Paris and speak French well. My chamber is small but very beautifully furnished—tho' you seldom see a carpet in Paris, the floors of the houses being made of oak finely polished and waxed or of little tiles painted red. Indeed I think I could not be so well situated elsewhere, nor could I obtain a place where I should enjoy so great advantages for acquiring knowledge of the French language. If I had my chambers at a hotel I should have a thousand solitary hours, because I cannot speak French well enough to go into French society—but now if I wish to be alone I can shut myself up in my chamber—If I wish for society I can go at any hour into Madame's parlor—and talk my kind of French with her and her daughters,—besides the pleasure of hearing most delicious music. I do not know whether this situation of mine will in the long run be more expensive than one at a hotel. We pay thirty six dollars a month—for our board and rooms—and our washing about 50 cents a week. But at present it is not in my power to be more particular touching expenses—after I have resided here a* [while] *longer I can give you more information—which I shall not fail to give from time to time. Our house is finely situated for a student—within five minutes walk of the Public Lectures on all subjects—but a few steps from the Luxembourg gardens and the Pantheon. I have reserved all description of persons—places and things in general until I have seen more of the city, and have had time to collect my thoughts a little, which are altogether in confusion from the total novelty of everything about me. I feel as happy as possible—am in the best health in the world—and delighted with Paris—where a person if he pleases can keep out of vice as well as elsewhere, tho' to be sure temptations are multiplied a thousand fold if he is willing to enter into them. Remembering me very kindly and affectionately to all.*

Early in 1826, before Henry traveled to Europe, his father, along with a number of other residents, incorporated the Portland Athenaeum. The organization purchased the Portland Library for $1,640.22. The original library was called the Falmouth Library, established in 1763. Portland was called Falmouth at that time and was still part of Massachusetts. Historian William Willis wrote of the beginnings of the library (you will see Henry's grandfather's name listed):

In 1763, several gentleman…desirous of promoting the diffusion of useful knowledge, and extending the means of information, made some attempts to establish a library. In 1765…the first associates were Enoch Freeman, Benjamin Titcomb, Stephen Longfellow, Richard Codman, Edward Watts, Thomas Scales, Paul Prince, John Waite, Benjamin Waite, Enoch Ilsley, Jonathan Webb, Francis Waldo, Thomas Smith, Moses Pearson, James Gooding, Josiah Noyes, John Cox, Jeremiah Pote, Alexander Ross, Ebenezer Mayo, John Wiswall, Richard King, Jedediah Preble, Ephraim Jones, Stephen Waite, and John Waite, Jr.…At the opening of the library in 1766, it contained but 93 volumes…not one was printed in this country…. We believe this to have been the first establishment of the kind in Maine. Not much addition was made to the books previous to the revolution.

During the American Revolution, the town of Falmouth was attacked by the British, who destroyed the old town home that housed the public library. Willis noted, "In the destruction of the town, the little collection was widely dispersed and a number of the books lost: during the war its operations were entirely suspended until 1780."

On February 28, 1826, the local newspaper, the *Eastern Argus*, reported of the Portland Athenaeum:

Such an institution has long been a desideratum among us. Other towns inferior to this in size and wealth have gone before us in the career of literary enterprize…and yet we are not willing to allow that there is any lack of literary elements in the town, but they lie scattered and dormant. There is no common centre of gravity to bring them into healthful action; they are like coals lying asunder which give no heat. We have scholars in town…but their lights are hid under a bushel…. We want an institution which shall bring them in contact, and give them the benefit of mutual light and heat, and action…. [It] shall combine a reading-room, a library and cabint…. it is contemplated to unite, if practicable, the two reading-rooms now open in town, together with the Portland Library.

By October 1864, the number of bound volumes had reached 10,647, besides a collection of pamphlets. The collection was lost to fire in 1866.

In July, Henry wrote to his brother Stephen from Paris, telling of his supposed new attire:

After five weeks' residence in Paris I have settled down something half-way between a Frenchman and a New Englander:—within,—all Jonathan—but outwardly a little of the Parlez-vous. That is to say, I have good home-feelings at heart—but have decorated my outwardly man with a long-waisted thin coat—claret-coloured—and a pair of linen pantaloons:—and on Sundays and other fete-days—I appear in all glory of a little hard French hat—glossy—brushed—and rolled—and rolled up at the sides.

Following is an excerpt from a letter that Henry's father had written to his son regarding dress:

It seems that you have changed your costume to that of a Parisian. You will allow me to doubt the expediency of confirming your dress to the fashion of the country in which you may reside for a short time. You will find it expensive to you, as your French dress would be useless to you in Spain or any other country, for an American in Spain, Italy, or Germany decked out in dress of a Frenchman will exhibit a very singular appearance. You should remember that you are an American, and as you are a visitor for a short time only in a place, you should retain your own national costume. You will find it much more convenient and less expensive.

Stephen did not keep Henry's letter a secret; Henry would later dismiss the letter about his attire as a playful joke.

In August, Henry left the residence of Madame Potet, complaining to his father that the other Americans who were also staying with her were speaking mostly English and not speaking enough French. In a letter to his father, Henry also explained his departure from Paris:

> *I found at length a young French gentleman who was my fellow passenger from America—who recommended me to the house in which I am at present residing. It is what in the language of the country is called a "Maison de santé" or "house of health"—where, retired from the noise and dust of the city, valatudinarians can breath the country air and become healed of their infirmities. Attached to the house is an extensive garden full of fruit trees—and bowers, and alcoves, where boarders ramble and talk from morning till night. This makes the situation an excellent one for me, for I can at anytime hear French conversation—for the French are always talking. Besides the conversation is the purest of French—inasmuch as persons from the highest circles in Paris are residing here.*

Henry had arrived in Paris on Sunday, June 18, 1826. By October, he had realized how difficult the French language would be to master. He remained in Paris through the New Year's celebration of 1927, writing to his sisters of New Year's Day in Paris, calling it a day of great gaiety and rejoicing and a holiday for all classes of people. By mid-February, Henry had not mastered the language but was very satisfied with the knowledge that he had acquired of it. To his father he wrote, "I am confident that I have done well. I cannot imagine who told you that six months was enough for the French—he would have been more correct if he said six years—that is—speaking of perfection in the language."

Henry left Paris for Spain, traveling by stagecoaches. He wrote to his father of Bordeaux and his travels:

> *In sober sadness—I had a most cold and uncomfortable ride of it:—and I assure you I felt my heart leap within me, when I heard the horses' hoofs clatter upon the stone bridge of Bordeaux. This is the most beautiful city I have seen in France. The climate, I think must be delicious—for to day, when you [are] shivering over the brands of a huge wood fire—around me the breath of Spring is breathing with a freshness to renovate the departed strength of Old age. But the spring—they say—is a tardy one—and not a*

Peleg Wadsworth's deed of the land to Stephen Longfellow, Portland, 1827. *Courtesy of the Collections of Maine Historical Society.*

tree has yet put its leaf. The city situated on the left bank of the Garonne, which sweeps away to the northward in a long regular curve:—and the houses upon the quai from arc of a circle—concave towards the city. From the bridge—one of the finest in France, it is said; you get a fine front view of the place; and on either side of you the eye rests upon the thick forest of Mast—the best kind of forest that a commercial town can be surrounded with. The public walks of the city are numerous and Beautiful;—and the commerce of all kinds carried on here gives the place an air of life and activity delightful to a traveller. The population is 91,000.—Thus you see me on my way to Spain. I shall leave this city for Madrid.

In Portland in 1827, Henry's father purchased land from his father-in-law, Peleg Wadsworth; the deed conveyed land to Stephen Longfellow on

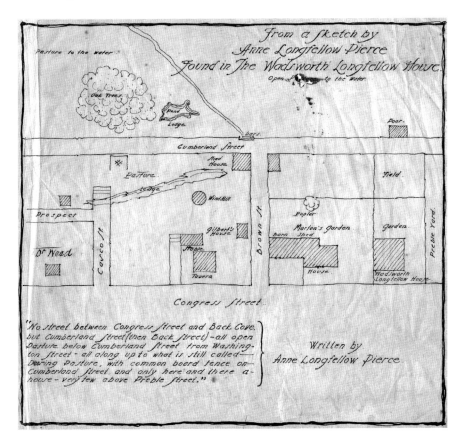

Sketch of the Longfellow house and its surroundings as they looked during Anne's childhood. *Courtesy of the Collections of Maine Historical Society.*

Cumberland Street in Portland for the sum of $1,110. The image here was a drawing done by Anne Longfellow, showing Cumberland Street and the land in back of the Longfellow house.

Henry arrived in Spain on February 27, the day of his twentieth birthday. He traveled to Segovia, which was a mountainous area northwest of Madrid, and then to Escoria; he would arrive back in Madrid in mid-March. While in Madrid, Henry stayed at the home of Señor Don Valentin Gonzalez along with his wife and daughter, Florencia.

While in Madrid, Henry met Washington Irving. Henry had been a fan of his work since he was a child. Later, he would recall the impression that *The Sketch Book* had made on him the first time he read the book. Irving had been in Madrid for more than a year when they first met, having been invited by United States ambassador Alexander H. Everett. The purpose of the invitation was so Irving could translate Navarette's book on the voyages of Columbus. To defer Irving's expenses for travel, he was made an attaché of the legation. A letter of introduction to Washington Irving was given to Henry by Pierre Irving, a relative whom Henry knew in Paris. Henry also carried letters to Irving.

Henry and Irving had a friendly relationship together, and Henry would follow Irving's work ethic by starting at 6:00 a.m. to work. Irving had told Henry, "I am always at work as early as six."

Henry traveled to El Pardillo with the Gonzalez family and later on his own to the south of Spain, traveling to Seville and the port city of Cadiz, where he would write a long letter to Washington Irving telling of his travels:

> *It was my intension to have written you from Seville, but I was there so short a time, and that short time was so fully occupied, that I found it impossible to fulfill that intension. I can assure you that that day which saw me safely entering the gates of Seville was a jubilee for me. I have been fortunate enough thus far to have escaped robbery and bloody murder;—and no wooden cross by the way side designates my burial place, nor melancholy pile of stones cries aloud of Spanish blood-guiltiness. I hope you will be as fortunate as I have been.*
>
> *At Seville, you will find very good accom[m]odations in the "Fonda de los Americanos—Calle de la Sierpe"—the No. I have forgotten—but you will easily find it. You may live there for 12 reals a day—and very well, too. From Seville you will take the Steam boat to this city. You will find the price at the hotels exorbitant. As soon as I landed I went up into the principle street and enquired for a Casa de Pupilos—in plain English,*

boarding house—and was fortunate enough to find one which suits me exactly. I have the most delightful chambers, that you can imagine. A neat bed chamber and a sitting room—that looks out upon the principle square of the city—with a fine sea-breeze coming past window during the day. The house is situated "Plaza de San Antonio No 4. Piso alto"—kept by "la Senora Lopez." If you are not fond of upper stories I find that in the lower stories of the same house there are also chambers to let.

Traveling from Cadiz to Gibralter, Henry arrived in Marseilles in December and, on New Year's Day 1828, in Florence, Italy, first stopping in Genoa, Italy. From Florence, Henry would write to his father concerning his expenses:

In Gibraltar I wrote you an account of my expenditures up to the date of that letter. But that there be no mistake—nor misunderstanding from the miscarriage of letters, I will copy from my book the amount of my expenditures, and the Bankers upon whom I have drawn by order of Messrs. Welles & co.

Paris—Rec. from	*Messrs. Welles. &co.*	*frcs 2300*
At Bayonne	*Messrs. Garcia &co.*	*" 200*
" Madrid from	*Messrs Adoin Garia &co.*	*$400*
" Seville "	*Peter Garcia*	*" 50*
" Gibraltar "	*Messrs Lagrave & Lapoutide*	*" 200*
" Marseilles "	*Messrs. Fitch Brothers &co*	*frcs 500*

frcs 3000. And $650

This gives you an exact view of my expenses up to the first of January 1928. I should think it best to make all remittances to Messrs. Welles &co. Their correspondence is so very extensive, and the firm on so safe footing— that it is not only the most convenient but the surest mode of placing funds in my hands:—so in a word, whether I be in Italy or Germany—be kind enough to forward all letters and bills to those gentlemen. I have only to add, that tho' I find travelling and residing in foreign countries very expensive, I make it my object to live as cheap as I can.

Samuel Welles served as Henry's banker and general agent while Henry traveled throughout Europe. Welles was an American with connections to Europe's first banking houses and United States banks.

While in Florence, Henry met through letters of introduction Princess Charlotte, the daughter of Joseph Bonaparte. The princess was married to Prince Napoleon, who was the son of Louis, former king of Holland. The Countess of Survilliers, wife of Joseph Bonaparte, was also present at the evening event. The Duchess of Istria was in attendance as well—a French beauty, as Henry wrote of her. The duchess, the former Marie-Jeanne Lapeyiere, married Jean-Baptiste Bessieres in 1801. Bessieres was a marshal of France who received the title of Duke of Istria from Napoleon in 1809. The next day, Henry dined with the Countess of Survilliers, and later, Princess Charlotte would play "Yankee Doodle" for Henry.

Henry left Florence for Rome after only staying in Florence for one month, disliking the sound of the Tuscan pronunciation. When he arrived in Rome, he met up with his friend George Washington Greene. In April, Greene and Longfellow traveled to Naples. In a letter to his brother Stephen, Henry wrote of Naples:

It is just a fortnight to-day that I have been sojourning in this delightful land, in whose description poetry can mingle little of soft and beautiful imagery, which has not here a local habitation and a name. Indeed— you see nature here as it glows in painting and blooms in song:—not that nature is not more lovely in herself—than in the Poet's album and the Painter's sketch book:—but you find in the scenery of Naples those rich combinations—which, were they found everywhere, would make the world we live in, too much Paradise. My windows overlook the bay of Naples— and directly in front of me on the other side of the water rises the broken cone of Vesuvius—with a thin light cloud of smoke wreathing itself about its summit—and fading away into the blue of the atmosphere. The long curve of the sea shore is lined with white villages—beyond, the blue promontory of Sor[r]entum juts into the sea—and farther out lies the island of Caprea.

Longfellow and Greene visited Mount Vesuvius and the ruins of Pompeii and continued to travel through southern Italy. Henry returned to Rome and continued to stay at the home of the Persiani family, while Greene continued to travel across southern France to Spain. Henry was quite fond of the oldest daughter of the Persianis, Julia. But he left Rome in December 1928 after receiving word from his father that Bowdoin had withdrawn his professorship position and changed it to that of an instructor, with an attendant reduction in pay. In a letter dated December 19, Henry wrote to his father from Venice, Italy:

On receiving yours of the 15th of September, I left Rome immediately. I unsealed your letter with the usual delightful feelings of hearing from home: but I assure you the perusal of it caused me great pain. The tidings that the anticipated appointment at Bowdoin has been refused me, were very unexpected and very jarring to my feelings. And more so, because it was a situation, which neither yourself, nor I, had solicited, but which had been gratuitously offered me upon certain conditions—the which I have scrupulously fulfilled. I assure you—my dear father—I am very indignant at this. They say I am too young! Were they not aware of this three years ago? If I am not capable of preforming the duties of the office, they may be very sure of my not accepting it. I know not in what light they may look upon it, but for my own part I do not in the least regard it as a favor conferred upon me. It is no sinecure: and if my services are an equivalent to my salary,—there is no favor done me:—if they be not, I do not desire the situation. If they think I would accept the place they offer me,—as I presume they do,—they are much mistaken in my character. No Sir—I am not yet reduced to this. I am not a dog to eat the crumbs, that fall from such a table.

Henry made his way to Dresden, Germany, with several letters of introduction from Washington Irving, who suggested that Henry study there. But after only a short time in Dresden, he left for Gottingen, arriving there on February 20. His good friend from Portland Ned Preble was already in Gottingen studying the German language. Henry was quite impressed with the library at the University of Gottingen, commenting that it was the largest in Germany, full of choice, rare works. Gottingen was a small city. Henry said that "there is no alternative but study." While Henry was in Gottingen, he received news of changes being made at the home in Portland. In 1814, after a fire in Henry's father's law office, the office was moved into the Portland home.

Built next to the room that was used as a dining/sitting room was a small room used primarily as a waiting room, but when not in use, Henry would use it as a study. Henry's mother decided to turn the room into a china closet. In a letter to his sister Elizabeth, Henry responded to the changes to the Portland home: "[N]o soft poetic ray has irradiated my heart—since the Goths and Vandals swept over the Rubicon of the 'front entry' and turned the Sanctum Sanctorum of the Little Room into a China Closet." By then, Henry had been in Europe for three years.

In excerpts from a letter to his mother, Henry wrote of his time in Europe and recent travels:

It is to day three years since I left America. In running my eye over this lapse of time, it seems to me more like an interlude in the drama of life, than a part of the play. I have just returned to Gottingen from a journey through Flanders to London and back by the way of Holland. With a map you may easily trace my course. From Gottingen I went to Cassel—thence to Frankfort—and to Mayence. At Mayence I took the steamboat on the Rhine: for they are told in tales and sung in ballads. It is a noble river: but no so fine as the Hudson. The ruins of old castles and monasteries which look down upon it from every eminence along its banks, give it a most picturesque appearance. The most beautiful and sublime scene is at the Bingerloch—the Highlands of the Rhine. It is there the river makes is great bend. The Nahe empties into it at the same spot,—and at their junction stands the beautiful village of Bingen. The river rushes in shallow rapids round the bend, and below spreads out into a long silver sheet—over which looks the most beautiful ruin of the Rhine. It is the old castle of Vautsberg—and stands upon the edge of a rugged precipice several hundred feet high, overhanging the river. I never saw a more picturesque object: and seldom a more lovely view.

After receiving the news of his sister Elizabeth's death, Henry boarded the ship *Manchester* in Liverpool, England. He wrote to his father on the day of his arrival in New York on August 11, 1829, "I have the pleasure of informing you of my safe return to my native land."

Back home, the Abyssinian Religious Society had been formed and incorporated in Portland in 1828. The society was started because six black citizens were protesting their treatment as churchgoers at the Second Congregational Church in Portland. A letter was published on September 19, 1826, in the *Eastern Argus* newspaper:

To the Public: the undersigning in behalf of themselves and their brethren would respectfully address themselves to the citizens of Portland. Their object is to solicit the kind attention of the benevolent, the pious, and the humane to the moral and religious condition of their people settled in this place. We know and feel that there is little in our situation in society, which is calculated to induce us to merit the approbation of the wise and the good. The Cheering and benign influences of those motives of action, which addresses themselves so powerfully to the feelings of the community around us, are shut out from us, and never penetrate our atmosphere to stimulate and encourage the children of our race. We allude with emotion to these considerations, as some apology for the vice and degradation, with which our people are charged—and we allude to them with the view of enforcing the peculiar importance of affording us moral instruction, and fortifying our minds with principles and sanctions of piety and religion. Our numbers amount to about six hundred. Provision for the accommodation of a very few of our people is made in several houses of public of public worship; but while the provision is totally inadequate to our wants, the privilege granted us is associated with such circumstances, calculated to repel rather than to invite our attendance. Nay, pardon our misapprehensions if they be such, we have sometimes thought our attendance was not desired. The undersigned are persuaded that nothing would so much contribute to improve the character and raise the ton of moral feeling among their people, as the erection for their use of a suitable house for public worship, and the regular ministration of the gospel. They cannot but consider the accomplishment of this objective as intimately and vitally connected with the usefulness and happiness of their people. It is an object, the undersigned have much at heart, and to promote which they and their brethren are ready to appropriate a portion of their very limited means. And they hope they shall not be thought obtrusive in taking this method of inviting the attention, and soliciting the aid and encouragement of the well disposed.

The six citizens were Reuben Ruby, Caleb Johnson, Clemant Tomson, Job L. Wentworth, Christian C. Manuel and John Siggs.

THE POET'S PROFESSORSHIP

On August 27, 1829, Henry wrote a letter to Bowdoin College's president, William Allen:

> *Your letter to my father, dated Sept. 26,1829, and enclosing a copy of the vote of the Trustees and Overseers of Bowdoin College, by which they have elected me Instructor of Modern Languages in that institution, has been duly handed me. I am sorry, that under existing circumstances, I cannot accept the appointment. The Professor of Modern Languages, with a salary equal to that of the other Professors, would certainly not have been refused. But having at great expense, devoted four years to the acquisition of the French, Spanish, Italian, and German, languages, I cannot accept a subordinate station with a salary so disproportionate to the duties required.*

The Bowdoin College trustees and overseers responded with an offer of the position of professor of modern languages with a salary of $800, $200 less than that paid to other professors. But the offer included an extra $100 to become the librarian for one hour per day. Henry accepted the position: "In answer to your communication this morning, announcing to me the vote of the Trustees and Overseers of Bowdoin College, by which I have been elected Professor of Modern Languages in that institution, I have the honor of informing you—that I willingly accept the appointment." At twenty-two years of age, Henry Wadsworth Longfellow was the professor of the new

A portrait painting of Henry Wadsworth Longfellow, circa 1829. *Courtesy of the Collections of Maine Historical Society.*

department of modern languages. For his first year at the college, he would only teach the languages of Spanish and French.

In Portland in 1829, Bowdoin college graduate Seba Smith (class of 1818) would start two nonpartisan newspapers: the *Portland Courier*, the first daily newspaper north and east of Boston, and the *Family Reader*, a weekly newspaper. Work on the Cumberland and Oxford Canal continued, connecting the waters of Sebago Lake to Portland Harbor.

Shortly after Maine's statehood, Portland's export market began expanding rapidly, and it became necessary to find a way to move goods to and from the coast. The ultimate solution was a canal running from the interior of the state to Portland. After a few false starts, a group of merchants was given a charter, fundraising was successful and construction began in earnest. The route ran from Oxford County, through Sebago Lake to Portland, a distance of about fifty miles. Travel was done by the use of specially built canalboats. On June 1, 1830, with great fanfare, the Cumberland and Oxford Canal was officially opened, but its use was very short-lived with the coming of the railroads that left canal shipping unprofitable.

Henry's brother Stephen took a private position as secretary to Judge William Pitt Preble, who had accepted the appointment as the ambassador extraordinary to The Hague. Stephen left Portland in December 1829. Henry wrote to him on the twenty-third of the month, informing him that he would remain at the college in Brunswick for the holiday. He also wrote to his father, telling him of a new proposed plan for studies for the year:

> *The new arrangement puts a hard-laboring oar into my hands, and will give me three recitations per day, besides the hour occupied in the library.*
>
> *The Junior Class will as usual recite French every afternoon. The Senior's will have three recitations a week in French—and three in Spanish—at noon. The Sophomore Class will recite French every morning. This, you perceive, gives me three recitations per diem, through the week, Saturday afternoons excepted. Besides this, I am to have a private lesson in German: and the prospect before me seems thick-sown with occupations, promising me little leisure for my private studies, which account for my busy life the last term.*

Already beginning to follow the advice given to him by Washington Irving, Henry also drank a tumbler of milk with a whole egg in it, followed by a short walk in the shade. Henry's close friend George Washington Green was married in Paris, France, on January 3, 1830, to Carlotta Sforzosi from Italy. Henry, still a bachelor, wrote to Green in a letter dated April 13, 1830:

> *The treasures of the deep are not so precious*
> *As are the concealed comforts of a man*
> *Locked up in a woman's love.*

Henry wrote his own textbooks on *French Exercises* for the beginning students and for the Spanish students and also translated two Spanish stories, called "El Serrano de las Alpujarras" and "El Cuadro Misterioso,"

Shipwreck at Pond Cove, Cape Elizabeth, Maine, by Portland artist Charles Codman, circa 1830. *Courtesy of the Collections of Maine Historical Society.*

Portland Head Light, Cape Elizabeth, Maine, circa 1930. *Courtesy of the Collections of Maine Historical Society.*

by George Washington Montgomery, an American writer living in Spain. The books were printed in the late spring of 1830.

Also in 1830, a shipwreck took place at Pond Cove in Cape Elizabeth, Maine, not far from the Portland Head Light, which had been commissioned by President George Washington in 1791. By the 1790s, Portland was the sixth-busiest port in the country, and Portland's population reached more than 1,200 in 1830. Henry frequently visited the lighthouse and was inspired by the rocky coast, writing about it in his poetry:

"The Sea-Diver"

My way is on the bright blue sea,
  My sleep upon its rocking tide;
And many an eye has followed me
  Where billows clasp the worn seaside.

My plumage bears the crimson blush,
  When ocean by the sun is kissed!
When fades the evening's purple flush,
  My dark wing cleaves the silver mist.

Full many a fathom down beneath
  The bright arch of the splendid deep
My ear has heard the sea-shell breath
  O'er living myriads in their sleep.

They rested by the coral throne,
  And by the pearly diadem;
Where the pale sea-grape had o'rgrown
  The glorious dwelling made from them.

At night upon my storm-drench'd wing,
  I poised above a helmless bark,
And soon I saw the shattered thing
  Had passed away and left no mark.

And when the wind and storm were done,
  A ship, that had rode out the gale,
Sunk down, without a signal-gun,
  And none was left to tell the tale.

I saw the pomp of day depart—
  The cloud resign its golden crown,
When to the ocean's beating heart
  The sailor's wasted corse went down.

Peace be those whose graves are made
  Beneath the bright and silver sea!
Peace—that their relics there were laid
  With no vain pride and pageantry.

Mary Storer Potter was one of the three daughters of Barrett Potter, a widower. He was the judge of probate, Cumberland County. Henry's father and Judge Potter were friends, and Henry knew Mary from the Portland Academy, where she was a younger schoolmate of his. Henry was interested in Mary and vice versa. He would have his sister Anne smuggle letters to Mary, for the judge kept a watchful eye over his daughters. Henry wrote to Anne, referring to Mary Potter as the "Captain": "I only call to leave a letter for the Captain, who has had the goodness to send me a ticket for the Ball tomorrow evening—for which I very much obliged. This however you will keep secret from everyone, even George Peirce himself. For I fancy that if the Judge finds out that I have written a letter to his daughter, he will stand on the defensive. So please hand it to her ladyship when no one is nigh—and she may do as she pleases about making it public."

George Washington Pierce would later marry Henry's sister Anne after a two-year engagement. Pierce was a graduate of Bowdoin College's class of 1825 with Henry and his brother Stephen. During the summer courtship and into the early fall of 1830, before the new term started at Bowdoin College, Henry and Mary became engaged. From Bowdoin College, Henry wrote to his future father-in-law:

> *I regretted that I had not the opportunity of conversing with you before leaving town on Wednesday morning, but the hurry of departure rendered it impossible. I wished to express the grateful acknowledgment I owe you, for the confidence you have reposed in me in placing in my hands the happiness of a daughter, and in part your own. I most ardently hope, my dear sir, that you may never have the slightest occasion to think that your confidence has been misplaced. I certainly believe you will never have: and this belief is founded upon the attachment I feel for Mary, in whom I find the inestimable virtues of a pure heart and guideless disposition—qualities which not only excite an ardent affection, but which tend to make it as durable as it is ardent. I think I have formed a just estimate of the excellence of Mary's character.*

Henry went on to write of Mary's gentleness and innocent spirit, as well as how privileged he was to have engaged her affections.

Henry's second year of teaching began with a formal introduction as professor of modern languages, during which he would give an inaugural address to Bowdoin College, the president, the faculty, the trustees, the students and the guests. The lecture was on the origin and growth of languages of southern Europe and literature. Henry also delivered two other lectures on education to the Benevolent Society of Portland and a convention of teachers in Augusta. He also went on to write scholarly articles for the *North American Review* and the *New-England Magazine*, which was a literary periodical. Gray and Bowen of Boston published a second edition of Henry's *French Grammar*. His first book for Gray and Bowen was published in 1831, called *Le Ministre de Wakefield*.

With the heavy schedule of his teaching duties, leaving less time to write, Henry soon started to regret the choice he had made to teach. He wrote to his sister Anne only three weeks before his wedding of the wedding plans and his regret. Anne was not well and was staying at the home of the Pierce family in Baldwin, Maine. She was engaged to George Washington Pierce:

> *I hope to see you before long, and shall if possible before Commencement: but not in Portland: for I think the country air is everything for you now, and you must not come home till you have derived all possible benefit from your present situation. We would postpone the wedding, dear Anne, on your account, if circumstances would permit: but the vacation is but 3 weeks,—and we have now fixed the wedding-day in the second:—so that we shall have barely time to get comfortably settled in Brunswick, before I shall be forced to commence grinding in the knowledge mill again. You call it a dog's life: it is indeed—my dear Anne: I don't believe that I was born for such a lot. I have aimed higher than this: and cannot believe that all my aspirations are to terminate in the drudgery of a situation, which gives me no opportunity to distinguish myself, and in point of worldly gain, does not even pay me for my labor. Besides, one loses ground so fast in these out of the way places: the mind has no stimulus to exertion—grows sluggish in it's movements and narrow in it's sphere—and there's the end of man. We will see.*

Henry Wadsworth Longfellow and Mary Storer Potter were married on September 14, 1831, in Portland.

In 1831, the Portland Fire Department was established, and a stove was installed in the Longfellow house. Additionally, a committee was named for the preparation of a city charter, which was approved by voters of Portland at the town meeting and was sent to the state legislature for approval.

Before their marriage, Henry searched the Brunswick area to find a suitable house where the couple could live but to no avail. Henry would remain with Mary at Mrs. Fale's boardinghouse, where he had been renting a few rooms. During this semester, Henry found more time to concentrate on other writing opportunities, although his teaching schedule was quite demanding, with four recitations per day. Henry worked on his *European Sketch Book* and for *New-England Magazine*, for which he translated Spanish poetry for publication. He also did one prose sketch and one short Spanish poem that was translated for *The Token*, a gift book annual edited by S.G. Goodrich.

From the period of September to December 1831, only two letters written by Henry are available, both to his sister Mary. In January 1832, Henry and his wife traveled to Boston and Cambridge. There he met Charles Folsom, an editor for the University Press. Over the next year, they would stay in close contact regarding Henry's publications of his grammar and readers. In March, Henry wrote to his publishers, Gray and Bowen, concerned that he had not heard back from Charles Folsom regarding his *Italian Reading Book*, which was still unfinished. In May, Henry visited Boston and Folsom in Cambridge. Returning to Bowdoin for the summer term, he wrote to his good friend George Washington Greene:

> *Yours of the 29th April has just reached me, on my arrival from Boston. What a misfortune has befallen me! To be so near you, and yet not to see you! To be within a half-day's journey to you, and yet not visit you! Why, if you had put your letter into the mail one day—one single day earlier, I should have received it a fortnight ago, and should have posted on to welcome your return to New England, in my own bodily presence, instead of sending you this sheet, blotted with pale ink and scrawled with a barbarous pen, from a chamber in the "Tontine hotel" of this village. Our vacation has just closed;—the summer term commenced today; and I returned to town this afternoon. Half the vacation I have passed in Boston, and as my time was wholly at my disposal, had I known of your return, I should have been in East Greenwich before the set of sun. Your letter is dated April 29th and bears the post mark May 18th it must have reached this place the same evening, that I left it for Portland. But adieu regrets!—let the past hold its peace and be still, whilst the voice of friendship welcomes you home again, and the future promises a happy meeting.*

This was quite a long letter to Greene, as he had suggested that Henry take a teaching position at University of New York, while Greene would take Henry's position at Bowdoin College. Henry was not happy with his position at the college and would continue to entertain other opportunities. In early July, Henry invited Greene and his wife to Brunswick. Henry was invited to deliver a poem for the Phi Beta Kappa Society of Bowdoin College at its annual fall meeting. In October 1832, Henry and wife, Mary, moved from Mrs. Fale's boardinghouse to a home on Federal Street in Brunswick. "It is one of the pleasantest in town, and one of the most convenient. It suits me exactly. The only thing that annoys me is the style of the paper-hangings, which cry aloud against the taste of my landlord and predecessor. Stripes of the most odious colors in all the parlors and chambers—and in the front entry green parrots dancing on the slack wire."

Charles Folsom had written to Henry earlier in the month with the official invitation to be Phi Beta Kappa poet at Harvard: "This appointment I would

Anne Longfellow Pierce, Portland, 1830. *Courtesy of the Collections of Maine Historical Society.*

Left: Silhouette portrait of George Washington Pierce, circa 1832. *Courtesy of the Collections of Maine Historical Society.*

Below: Panorama, *S.E. View of Portland*, 1832, by Pendleton's Lithography, Boston. *Courtesy of the Collections of Maine Historical Society.*

privately as a friend urge on you to accept…Again I repeat it, as a friend, I think you ought to accept this present appointment."

Henry responded, "I accept the appointment with much pleasure, and of course shall endeavor so to demean myself as to give you no cause to regret your friendly intervention in my behalf." Henry would have a year to prepare for the event.

In Portland on November 26, 1832, Henry's sister Anne married George Washington Pierce. Also in 1832, the state capital was moved from Portland to Augusta. Portland had been the capital since 1820, when Maine was separated from Massachusetts and admitted into the Union. At the time, it was practical for Portland to be the home of the state's government because of its larger population and ready-made facilities for larger meeting space. But by 1832, population had been spreading throughout the state, and it was becoming an inconvenience for legislative members to travel the sometimes great distances for sessions. Hence, the capital was moved.

As the school year continued, Henry contributed to *New-England Magazine* and others while working on a new work, *Outre-Mer*. When it was finished, Henry contacted Lilly, Wait and Company in Boston, which decided against printing the book, so Henry brought the manuscript to Griffin's Press in Brunswick. When it was completed, still no publisher had been found and the cover page had still not been printed, but by late June, Hilliard, Gray and Company had agreed to buy the book.

Still unhappy with his situation at Bowdoin, Henry looked into a possible position as a lecturing assistant to Professor Ticknor at Harvard or as the secretary of legation in Madrid, as well as opening a girls' school in New York—all to no avail.

In August 1833, Henry traveled by stage to Cambridge, where he delivered his poem "The Past and the Present" to the Harvard Phi Beta Kappa Society. Also on the platform was Edward Everett, who had replaced John Quincy Adams, who had been originally asked to speak. Henry wrote to Everett requesting a copy of his address. Upon receiving it, Henry wrote to Everett, "I had the pleasure of receiving a day or two since the copy of your Phi Beta Kappa Address, which you were kind enough to send me, and for which I beg you to receive my best acknowledgments. If a voice from the Far East can add anything to the general applause which has elsewhere greeted its appearance, be assured that we have read it here with feelings of delight and admiration." Everett was educated at Harvard, studied in Europe, taught ancient Greek literature at Harvard and was one of the great American orators.

Henry returned to Bowdoin to continue to teach Spanish, French and Italian using his own textbooks. For German, he did not.

The *New York Atlas* and *Constellation* were printing excerpts from *Outre-Mer* in their weekly editions. Henry was accused of plagiarism by a reader signed "John" and wrote to the editor of the publication in defense of his work:

> *I am much obliged to you for your kindness in sending me the last No. of your paper, in which I drew the incident of the tale of Martin Franc and the monk of St. Anthony. In the remarks preceding this tale in* Outre-Mer, *it was said to have come from "an ancient manuscript of the Middle Ages." Indeed, during the thirteenth century this story seems to have been very popular one: and several versions of it, each differing from the other in details of the narrative, are in existence.*

Henry went on to list a number of references where he found his information:

> *This may seem to be tracing up the matter far enough; but I must go one step farther the leading idea of the story was not original with the author of the Segretain Moine. He probably borrowed it from the East: for it is a fact pretty well established in literary History, that during the times of the Crusades, the early French Poets brought from the east many of the tales that make the ground-work of their poems. The Segretain Moine was doubtless drawn from The Story of the Little Hunchback, a tale of the Arabian Nights Entertainments. Thus the story has passed through as many hands as did the body of the Friar Gui. Mr. Colman evidently drew the incidents of The Knights and the friar from the same source whence I drew those of Martin Franc. Had I known of the existence of the former before the publication of the latter, I certainly should have left Mr. Colman undisputed possession of the field. Unfortunately I was not aware, till after the publication of Outre-Mer No. 1., that any modern writer had availed himself of this old fiction. In conclusion I would say, that I have never had any desire to conceal the origin of this tale. In this quarter it is quite an old story, inasmuch as the Professor you speak of has cited it in college lectures as a specimen of the fictions of the early poets of France. Give my best respects to John. His idea, that Colman borrowed the story from me, is ingenious. I can certainly say with truth, that he is as much indebted to me for it, as I am to him. When I next visit your city, I shall expect from John an invitation to the Club-room.*

In response, the *New York Atlas* and *Constellation* noted:

It now affords us great satisfaction and pleasure to acknowledge the kindness and urbanity of Prof. L. in sending us the subjoined letter from his own hand, in which he most conclusively vindicates himself, and at the same time enables us to do him the justice of repairing an unintentional injury, however trivial or unheeded. In no way can we do this so well as by allowing the amiable and ingenious professor to plead his justification in his own candid and happy manner. We therefore give his letter entire—believing he will forgive the freedom of substituting his private communication for any crude remarks of our own.

FROM OUTRE MER—*MARTIN FRANC AND THE MONK OF SAINT ANTHONY*

In times of old there lived in the city of Rouen a tradesman, Named Martin Franc, who by a series of misfortunes, had been reduced to opulence to poverty. But poverty, which generally makes men humble and laborious, only served to make him proud and lazy; and in proportion as he grew poorer and poorer, he grew also prouder and lazier. He contrived, however, to live along from day to day, by now and then pawning a silken robe of his wife, or selling a silver spoon, or some other trifle saved from the wreck of his better fortune; and passed his time pleasantly enough in loitering about the market place, and walking up and down on the sunny side of the street.

The fair Marguerite, his wife, was celebrated through the whole city for her beauty, her wit, and her virtue. She was a brunette, with the blackest eye—the whitest teeth—and the ripest nut brown cheek in all of Normandy;—her figure was tall and stately—her hands and feet most delicately moulded—and her swimming gate like motion of a swan. In happier days she had been the delight of the richest of tradesmen in the city, and the envy of the fairest dames; and when she became poor, her fame was not a little increased by her cruelty to several substantial burghers, who, without consulting their wives, had generously offered to stand between her husband and bankruptcy, and do all in their power to raise a worthy and respectable family. The friends of Martin Franc, like the friends of many a ruined man before and since, deserted him in the day of adversity. Of all that had eaten his dinners, and drunk his wine, and philandered with his wife, none sought the narrow alley and humble dwelling of the broken tradesman, save one; and that one was Friar Gui, the sacristan of the

Abbey of Saint Anthony. He was a little, jolly, red-faced friar, with leer in his eye, and a naughty reputation for a man of his cloth; but as he was a kind of travelling gazette and always brought the latest news and gossip of the city, and besides was the only person that condescended to visit the house of Martin Franc,—in fine, for the want of a better, he was considered in the light of a friend. In these constant assiduities, Friar Gui had his secret motives, of which the single heart of Martin Franc was entirely unsuspicious. The keener eye of his wife, however, soon discovered two faces under the hood. She observed that the Friar generally timed his visits so as to be at the house when Martin Franc was not at home,—that he seemed to prefer the edge of evening,—and that his visits became more frequent he always had some little apology ready, such as "being obliged to pass that way, he could not go by the door without just dropping in to see how good man Martin did."—occasionally, too, he ventured to bring her some ghostly present—such as a picture of the Madonna and child, or one of those little naked images, which are hawked about the streets at the Nativity. Though the object of all this was but too obvious, yet the fair Marguerite preserved in misconstruing the Friar's intension, and in dexterously turning aside any expressions of gallantry that fell from his venerable lips. In this way Friar Gui was for a long time kept at bay; and Martin Franc preserved in the day of poverty and distress, that consolation of all this world's afflictions—a friend. But finally things came to pass that the honest tradesman opened his eyes, and wondered he had been asleep so long. Whereupon he was irreverend enough to tweak the nose of Friar Gui, and then thrust him into the street by the shoulders. Meanwhile the times grew worse and worse. One family relic followed another;—the last silken robe was pawned—the last silver spoon sold.

February 1834 brought more disappointment as Henry was searching for a way out of Brunswick and Bowdoin College. He looked into renting the Round Hill School in Northampton, Massachusetts: "The spot is lovely indeed—lovely even beneath its mantle of snow. I have seen it in summer— and I believe it one of the most beautiful places in New England." After discussing the proposal with his most trusted friends in Boston and Portland, the idea was scrapped. "So that I consider the whole business as blown into thin air—and I awake as from a dream." But after almost a year, the dream opportunity arrived. Henry received a letter from Harvard president Josiah Quincy informing him of the retirement of Professor Ticknor and the offer to become Professor Ticknor's successor. Henry did not accept immediately, but eventually he would take the position at Harvard. He was formally elected on November 17, 1836, to the Smith Professorship of Modern Languages.

Before beginning his teaching duties at Harvard, Henry first resigned from Bowdoin College as its professor of modern languages and librarian. Henry then traveled abroad to strengthen his language skills. In a letter dated March 21, 1835, to his friend George Washington Greene, he discussed his travel plans:

> *I expected to have ere this in Boston but having heard that the Hannibal, which sails on the 1ˢᵗ April, and in which I had intended to take passage, is an inferior vessel both in her speed and accommodations, I have concluded to wait until the 16ᵗʰ, and take the Philadelphia for London. This will give me more time in Boston and New York—a circumstance much to be desired, in order to obtain letters &c. &c. I have concluded you see to go first to London. I shall remain there two or three weeks, and then make the best of my way to Stockholm, where I shall remain until October. The winter will be passed in Berlin—and the succeeding summer in Copenhagen. This is in brief the plan of my journey.*

The Longfellows would not travel alone. Joining them on their journey were two ladies from Boston: Mary Goddard and Clara Crowninshield. They all left America on April 10, 1835, from New York. On April 9, Henry wrote to his father:

> *We set our trunks on board ship,—she has hauled off into the stream—and we are only waiting for the morning to go on board. The weather to-day is lovely and like summer. We hope to have a pleasant day tomorrow. We sail in the ship Philadelphia—Capt. Morgan, a very pleasant and good-natured man; who promises to take us to London in three weeks. If he is longer than that, he shall call it a long passage and feel badly about it. The accommodation of the ship are very good—the state rooms large—and the cabin airy.*

They reached London on May 8, staying there for a month before moving on through Germany and Denmark to Stockholm, Sweden.

Mary Longfellow was pregnant and not in the best of health. After two months in Stockholm, they moved on to Copenhagen, Denmark. The group was reduced to three when Mary Goddard received word of the death of William Warren Goddard. Mary Goddard left for London and

Portrait sketch of Henry Wadsworth Longfellow by Maria Christiana Rohl, a popular Danish portrait artist. *Courtesy of the National Park Service, Longfellow House, Washington's Headquarters National Historic Site.*

boarded the ship *Philadelphia* to New York. From Rotterdam, Holland, Henry wrote to Mary Goddard's family, "We are very anxious to hear of Mary's safe arrival. She was so much afflicted by the melancholy news we received at Copenhagen, and expressed so strong a desire to return home, that I could not advise her to act otherwise than her heart prompted her. Under Mr. Appleton's charge she went safely to London;—and I doubt not has reached you in safety." John James Appleton and Henry met in

From the Eastern Argus of Monday. Nov. 16. 1835

"In the midst of life, we are in death".
Melancholy, indeed, and heart-rending, is the
illustration of this solemn truth — now furnished
to us and this community, in the death of
a fellow-citizen — that we are called upon
to announce.

George W. Pierce, Esq. of this city,
died at his residence, on Cumberland street,
yesterday morning at about 7 o'clock, after
a painful illness somewhat exceeding four
weeks duration, aged 30 years within a few
days.

We may truly say, that never has the
demise of any young man in this city,
or even elsewhere, been calculated to arouse
the sympathies of friends, and to fill
every mind with deep and impressive
regrets, more vividly than does the death
of the lamented subject of this notice.

George Washington Pierce obituary, Portland, 1835. *Courtesy of the Collections of Maine Historical Society.*

Stockholm. Appleton had served twice as American charge d' affaires to Sweden.

While in Rotterdam, Mary Longfellow had a miscarriage. Her health did not improve, and on November 29, 1835, Mary passed away. On December 1, Henry wrote a letter to Barrett Potter with the news of the death of his daughter.

Henry had her body shipped to America and then left Rotterdam with his travel companion Clara Crowninshield for Heidelberg, Germany. While in Germany, he could not concentrate on his studies while mourning the death of his wife. To make matters worse, Henry received word from home

Profile portrait of Henry Wadsworth Longfellow, 1835. *Courtesy of the George J. Mitchell Department of Special Collections and Archives, Bowdoin College Library, Brunswick, Maine.*

informing him of the death of his sister Anne's husband, George Washington Pierce. Henry was very close to his brother in-law. They were friends and graduated from Bowdoin College together. Henry wrote to his father on his friend's death, "The news of George's sickness and death was very sudden and unexpected. I warmly sympathize with you all, and in particular with Anne in this great affliction; and desire most ardently to be with you once more. At most, it will not be long;—only a few months after this letter reaches you. And thus will end a tour which has been productive of very little pleasure and much pain."

Henry decided to go to Italy to visit his good friend George Washington Greene but was turned away at the Italian border for improper documentation. He traveled alone to Switzerland, as his travel companion Clara remained in Heidelberg. As Henry traveled throughout Switzerland, he was introduced to the Appleton family from Boston. Nathan Appleton was a widower traveling with his two daughters, Mary and Frances; his son, Tom; and their cousins, William Appleton and Isaac Appleton Jewett. They had been traveling throughout Europe for about a year, part of a two-year trip. Henry was invited to join the Appletons on their journey, and for a brief period, he did travel with the family, enjoying the time he spent with the two sisters. As the time passed by, he became quite taken by the daughter Frances (Fanny), writing in his journal, "Read Uhland and Count Auersberg till dinner. After dinner walked with Miss Fanny."

Henry received a letter from Clara Crowninshield (one of his original travel companions) requesting his return to Heidelberg in order to escort her back to America. He wrote to his father:

> *I wrote you last from Geneva: from which place I returned to Heidelberg, where I remained only long enough to make the necessary arrangements for our return, and we are already thus far on our way back. We shall sail from Harve on the 8th of October, in the Silvie de Grace. This is the first good vessel; and is one of the best in the line. I hope therefore to be with you as early as the middle of November; quick passages being made in October.*

THE POET AT HARVARD

Henry arrived in Cambridge in 1836 to prepare for his professorship at Harvard. He was able to find lodging at the home of Dr. Sterns, another professor, on Kirkland Street. Henry wrote to his good friend George Washington Greene, "I have a nest not unlike the birds, being high up—in the third story." But remember that it was high up on the third floor of his childhood home in Portland where young Longfellow was so inspired by the sounds of the sea that he could hear from his window and the view of the small town at night leading down to the harbor:

"The Harvest Moon"

It is the Harvest Moon! On gilded vanes
  And the roofs of villages, on woodland crest
  And their aerial neighborhoods of nest
  Deserted, on the curtained window-panes
  Of rooms where children sleep, on country lanes
  And harvest-fields, its mystic splendor rest!
  Gone are the birds that were our summer guest;
  With the last sheaves return the laboring wains!
  All things are symbols: the external shows
  Of nature have their image in the mind
  As flowers and fruits and falling of the leaves:
  The song-birds leave us at the summer's close.
  Only the empty nest are left behind.
  And pipings of the quail among the sheaves.

His duties at the college were not set to begin immediately, giving him time to settle in. With this extra time, he would prepare a number of lectures on European literature for the spring term. Henry's father wrote to him about his new role at Harvard:

> *I rejoice, my dear son, that you are at length established in so very eligible a situation. With your literary tastes and habits, I can hardly conceive of a more pleasant location, and I most sincerely hope and pray it may remain permanent, and that no unfortunate circumstances may occur to mar your enjoyment or diminish your usefulness. I think your ambition must be satisfied, and your only object now will be to fill with eminence and distinction the office in which you are placed, and to become distinguished among the literary men of the age.*

Henry found his surroundings quite pleasing concerning his social life. He was welcomed into the society by his close friend Charles Folsom: "I am impatient as a lover to see you. Don't fail to come club at my house tonight with Mr. Felton." Cornelius Conway Felton was an American educator, professor of Greek literature at Harvard and later president and regent of the Smithsonian Institution. Felton and Longfellow would later team up with Henry Cleveland, an author and Harvard graduate, and Charles Sumner, an American lawyer, politician, orator, Massachusetts senator and a leader of the antislavery movement. Also joining the group was George Stillman Hillard, an American lawyer, author and Massachusetts legislator. They would refer to themselves as the Five of Clubs.

Henry's duties at Harvard included the management of the team of instructors that taught classes in German, Spanish, Italian and French and the preparation of lectures on linguistic and literary subjects. On May 23, 1837, he began giving his lectures at Harvard. He briefly wrote to his good friend George Washington Greene in Italy on the subject, "When did you see Ticknor last? Where is he now? When you next meet salute him friendly from me. Tell him the lectures of his successor commence in two days from this date." Professor George Ticknor was due to retire but would retain his office until Henry's return from Europe to begin the Smith Professorship at Harvard.

While in his first year at Harvard, Henry heard from his Bowdoin College classmate Nathaniel Hawthorne. Hawthorne had just written *Twice Told Tales*. Although they were not close friends at Bowdoin,

Hawthorne asked if Henry would review his book. Henry enjoyed the book and gave it a stunning review. "This book, though in prose, is written nevertheless by a poet."

In May 1837, a law student friend of Henry's who had been renting rooms at Craigie House in Cambridge was moving. During a visit there, Henry was introduced to Mrs. Craigie and inquired about renting. Mrs. Craigie was quick in remarking that she did not want to rent to any more students. Henry informed her that he was teaching at Harvard and the author of the book *Outre-Mer*, to which she replied that she owned a copy. After a tour of the house and learning of its rich history, Henry was even more interested. The home was built in 1759 by Major John Vassall. He had fled Cambridge at the beginning of the American Revolutionary War due to his loyalty to the king of England. The house had also been occupied by George Washington and was used as his headquarters from July 16, 1775, to April 4, 1776. Henry wrote to his father, "I intend to change my lodging. I have found two large and beautiful rooms in the Craigie-house, and thither I go at the close of the term. I shall be sorry to leave Mrs. Stearns on many accounts; But I cannot endure boarding homes. In the Craigie rooms, I shall be entirely my own master, and have

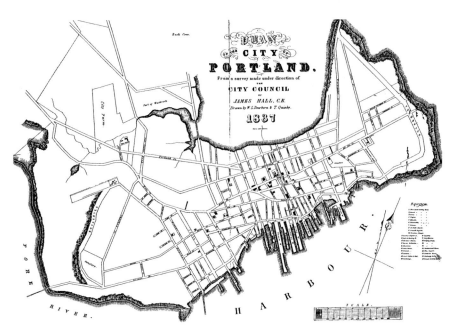

Plan of the city of Portland, 1837, by James Hall. *Courtesy of the Collections of Maine Historical Society.*

my meals by myself and at my own hours. So I form to myself a vision of independence, which I do not now enjoy."

Henry returned to Portland in August 1837 for a brief stay. In the image here of the plan of the city of Portland, on each end of the city, the Western and Eastern Promenades have been laid out, many new streets have been named and the forests are gone. Quite a change from the small town of Henry's past. As he often did, he remembered his early days in Portland in a poem, "A Gleam of Sunshine," which read in part:

> *This is the place. Stand still, my steed,*
> *Let me review the scene,*
> *And summon from the shadow Past*
> *The forms that once have been.*

> *The Past and Present here unite*
> *Beneath Time's flowing tide,*
> *Like footsteps hidden by a brook,*
> *But seen on either side.*

> *Here runs the highway to the town;*
> *There the green lane descends,*
> *Through which I walked to church with thee,*
> *O gentlest of my friends!*

While in Portland, Henry received a letter from Harvard president Josiah Quincy informing him of changes in his duties at the college. Respectfully, Henry replied with a counteroffer of sorts as to what he was willing to accept as changes to his schedule. A deal was struck, and the college and Henry were quite happy with the outcome. One oral lecture per week the year through, acting as superintendent of studies and instructors, being present at least once a month at the recitation of every student in each language and providing in the summer term two lectures on literature and literary history per week. If these duties were found to be too much, he would have the option of only doing one written lecture per week in the summer. To his father he wrote, "Thus everything is settled to my entire satisfaction; and I shall commence the term in great spirits, and lecture on the Faust of Gothe, of which I shall probably have an edition printed here—not at my own expense—which is something unusual."

View of the Whig Pavilion, Mount Joy, Portland, 1837, by Samuel Hodeson Colesworthy. *Courtesy of the Collections of Maine Historical Society.*

Henry was now settled at the Craigie House and quite happy. "In my new abode I dwell like an Italian Prince in his villa." He wrote to his sister Anne, "By the way—the frilled shirt is the queerest looking shirt, when on, you ever beheld. Stay thy hand: and wait till I come. I cannot tell you how to alter it—but can show you, anon. (Dickeys wanted: and likewise white linen handkerchiefs. Nothing else, if I remember right.)" Anne was a seamstress and often sent her brother handmade gifts. They had been very close since childhood: "Excuse my levity. I hate to [write] serious letters. I think it better to write nonsense: that is, sometimes."

The fall term went as well as Henry could have expected. The Appletons had returned in September, and Henry on occasion visited with Frances and wrote to her throughout the fall term. Henry returned to Portland in December for Christmas.

He wrote to George Washington Greene on January 6, 1838, "I saw in Switzerland and traveled with a fair lady—whom I now love passionately (strange, will this sound to yr. ears) and have loved ever since I knew her. A glorious and beautiful being—young—and a woman not of talent but of genius!—Indeed a most rare, sweet woman whose name is Fanny Appleton." Henry went on in this letter about the horrible fate that had fallen on him, "for Fanny lends no favorable ear to his passion, and for his love she gives only friendship." Henry vowed to win her affections.

In May of that year, Henry began a new course on Literature and the Literary Life. In June, he wrote a new poem, released in 1839 as part of *Voices of the Night*:

"The Psalm of Life"

Tell me not, in mournful numbers,
Life is but an empty dream!—
For the soul is dead that slumbers,
And things are not what they seem.

Life is real! Life is earnest!
And the grave is not its goal;
Dust thou art, to dust returnest,
Was not spoken of the soul.

Not enjoyment, and not sorrow,
Is our destined end or way;
But to act, that each to-morrow
Find us farther than to-day.

Art is long, and Time is fleeting,
And our hearts, though stout and brave,
Still, like muffled drums, are beating
Funeral marches to the grave.

In the world's broad field of battle,
In bivouac of Life,
Be not like dumb, driven cattle!
Be a hero in the strife!

Trust no Future, howe'er pleasant!
Let the dead Past bury its dead!
Act,—act in the living Present!
Heart within, and God o'erhead!

Lives of great men all remind us
We can make our lives sublime,
And, departing, leave behind us
Footprints on the sands of time;

Footprints, that perhaps another,
Sailing o'er life's solemn main,

A forlorn and shipwrecked brother,
  Seeing, shall take heart again.

Let us, then, be up and doing,
  With a heart for any fate;
Still achieving, still pursuing,
  Learn to labor and to wait.

Henry returned to his childhood home in Portland for the remainder of his summer vacation of 1838 while working on *Hyperion*. In his journal in September, he wrote, "Looked over my notes and papers for

Portrait of Henry Wadsworth Longfellow, 1839, by Belgian portrait painter Wilhelm Hendrik Franquinet. *Courtesy of the National Park Service, Longfellow House, Washington's Headquarters National Historic Site.*

Hyperion. Long for leisure to begin once more." Remarking on his schedule at Harvard, Henry wrote to George Washington Greene, "Meanwhile I labor and work right on with what heart and courage I may, and despite all sympathy; and am quite reasonably cool for a madman. I do a great deal in College; and devote all my hours to literature—morning, noon and night."

The year 1839 was one of much success, owing to the publication of both *Voices of the Night* and *Hyperion*:

> *From* Hyperion, *Book I, Chapter I*
> *"The Hero"*
>
> *The setting of a great hope is like the setting of the sun. The brightness of our life is gone. Shadows of evening fall around us, and the world seems but a dim reflection,—itself a broader shadow. We look forward into the coming, lonely night. The soul withdraws into itself. Then stars arise, and the night is holy. Paul Flemming had experienced this, though still young. The friend of his youth was dead. The bough had broken "under the burden of the unripe fruit." And when, after a season, he looked up again from the blindness of his sorrow, all things seemed unreal. Like a man, whose sight had been restored by miracle, he beheld men, as trees, walking. His household gods were broken. He had no home. His sympathies cried aloud from his desolate soul, and there came no answer from the busy, turbulent world around him. He did not willingly give way to grief. He struggled to be cheerful,—to be strong. But he could no longer look into the familiar faces of his friends. He could no longer live alone, where he had lived with her. He went abroad, that the sea might be between him and the grave. Alas! Between him and his sorrow there could be no sea, but that of time. He had already passed many months in lonely wandering, and was pursuing his way along the Rhine, to the south of Germany. He had journeyed the same way before, in brighter days and a brighter season of the year, in the may of life and in the month of May. He knew the beauteous river all by heart;—every rock and ruin, every echo, every legend. The ancient castles, grim and hoar, that had taken root as it were on the cliffs,—they were all his; for his thoughts dwelt in them, and the wind told him tales.*

From Hyperion, *Book III, Chapter IV*
"The Evening and the Morning Star"

Old Froissart tells us, in his Chronicles, that when King Edward beheld the
Countess of Salisbury at her castle gate, he thought he had never seen before
so noble nor so fair a lady; he was stricken therewith to the heart with a
sparkle of fine love, that endured long after; he thought no lady in the world
so worthy to be beloved, as she. And so likewise thought Paul Flemming,
when he beheld the English lady in the fair light of a summer morning. I
will not disguise the truth. She is my heroine; and I mean to describe her
with great truth and beauty, so that all shall be in love with her, and I most
of all. Mary Ashburton was in her twentieth summer. Like the fair maiden
Amoret, she was sitting in the lap of womanhood. They did her wrong,
who said she was not beautiful; and yet

> *"she was not fair,*
> *Nor beautiful;—those words express her not.*
> *But O, her looks had something excellent,*
> *That wants a name!"*

Her face had a wonderful fascination in it. It was such a calm, quiet face,
with the light of the rising soul shining so peacefully through it. At times
it wore an expression of seriousness,—of sorrow even; and then seemed to
make the very air bright with what the Italian poets so beautifully call the
lampeggiar dell' angelico riso,—the lightning of the angelic smile. And O,
those eyes—those deep, unutterable eyes, with "down-falling eyelids, full of
dreams and slumber," and within them a cold, living light, as in mountain
lakes at evening, or in the river of Paradise, forever gliding.

Frances Appleton was Mary Ashburton; Longfellow was Paul Flemming.

Johann Paul Friedrich Richter "Jean Paul" was a German Romantic writer, born in Wunsiedel, a town in the upper Franconian District of Wunsiedel in northeast Bavaria, Germany. *Hyperion* was written in the style of Jean Paul, who is spoken of in the book (Book 1, Chapter V, "Jean Paul, The Only-One"): "And all he does, is done with a kind of serious playfulness. He is a sea-monster, disporting himself on the broad ocean; his very sport is earnest; there is something majestic and serious about it. In everything there is strength, a rough good nature, all sunshine overhead, and underneath the heavy moaning of the sea. Well may he be called 'Jean Paul, the Only-One.'"

Henry wrote to George Washington Greene once *Hyperion* was finished: "I have written a Romance during the last year, into which I have put my feelings,—my hopes and sufferings for the last three years. Things are shadowed forth with distinctness enough to be understood; and yet mingled with fiction in the events set down as to raise doubt, and perplexity. The Feelings of the book are true;—the events of the story mostly fictitious. The heroine of course bears a resemblance to the lady, without being an exact portrait."

Henry sent a copy of *Hyperion* to the Appletons, and Fanny's reaction was silence on the subject, as she saw clearly through Henry's attempt at anonymity. She would only grow more distant, and her silence was heartbreaking to Henry.

In December 1839, Henry would discover that *Hyperion* had been on the market for three months, but about 1,200 copies were seized by the printers and binders as security for their notes. Henry's loss would be about $500. The books would be released in time.

Henry's belief in *Hyperion* never wavered, and neither did his love for Fanny. In 1841, he returned to his family's home in Portland, where he wrote the following due to the pain of the loss of loved ones over the years and the rejection of his love by Fanny:

"THE RAINY DAY"

The day is cold, and dark, and dreary;
It rains, and the wind is never weary;
The vine still clings to the mouldering wall,
But at every gust the dead leaves fall,
And the day is dark and dreary.

My life is cold, and dark, and dreary;
It rains, and the wind is never weary;
My thoughts still cling to the mouldering Past,
But the hopes of youth fall thick in the blast,
And the days are dark and dreary.

Be still, sad heart! And cease repining;
Behind the clouds is the sun still shining;
Thy fate is the common fate of all,
Into each life some rain must fall,
Some days must be dark and dreary.

Right: Henry Wadsworth Longfellow, 1840, by Cephas Giovanni Thompson. *Courtesy of the Collections of the Maine Historical Society.*

Below: Munjoy Hill in the 1840s. *Courtesy of the Collections of Maine Historical Society.*

"The Rainy Day" was published in 1842 as part of the collection called *Ballads and Other Poems.* Also included in this collection was the following poem:

"IT IS NOT ALWAYS MAY"

The sun is bright,—the air is clear,
   The darting swallows soar and sing,
And from stately elms I hear
   The bluebird prophesying Spring.

So blue yon winding river flows,
   It seems an outlet from the sky,
Where, waiting till the west wind blows,
   The freighted clouds at anchor lie.

All things are new:—the buds, the leaves,
   That gild the elm-tree's nodding crest,
And even the nest beneath the eaves;—
   There are no birds in last year's nest!

All things rejoice in youth and love,
   The fullness of their first delight!
And learn from the soft heavens above
   The melting tenderness of night.

Maiden, that read'st this simple rhyme,
   Enjoy thy youth, it will not stay;
Enjoy the fragrance of thy prime,
   For oh, it is not always May!

Enjoy the Spring of Love and Youth,
   To some good angel leave the rest;
For Time will teach thee soon the truth,
   There are no birds in last year's nest!

In the ending of *Hyperion,* Henry wrote:

It was daylight; and he heard the postilion, and the stamping of horses'
hoofs on the pavement at the door. At the same moment his servant came

in, with coffee, and told him all was ready. He did not dare to stay. But, throwing himself into the carriage, he cast one look towards the window of the Dark Ladie, and a moment afterwards had left her forever! He had drunk the last drop of the bitter cup, and now laid the golden goblet gently down, knowing that he should behold it no more! No more! O how majestically mournful are those words! They sound like the roar of the wind through a forest of pines! **The End**.

The story for Henry, however, would not end as it did for Paul Flemming in *Hyperion*. On July 13, 1843, Henry finally married Frances Appleton. The sketchbook that she had made while in Switzerland, when they had first met, was a wedding gift to Henry, signed, "To Paul Flemming from Mary Ashburton." Longfellow's career soared to heights in the literary world well beyond his expectations. The Fireside Poets was a group of poets who used a similar method of writing time and included William Cullen Bryant, James Russell Lowell, Oliver Wendell Holmes Sr., John Greenleaf Whittier and Henry Wadsworth Longfellow. These poets used the practice of standard forms, regular meter and rhymed stanzas, making the poetry easy to memorize and recite. These American poets were popular abroad as well as in America, rivaling that of the British poets who were so well accepted by the American and British public. The subjects, simple at times, made the poetry a form of entertainment for families gathered around warm, cozy fires.

SISTER ANNE

Anne Longfellow Pierce left the home to the Maine Historical Society upon her death in 1901. She had made a list of instructions for the contents of the house—some of the items were to be given to family, and others were to remain in the location where they had been during Henry's life in the home. This is just a sample of her instructions:

> *Fathers chair to be left in the room with the table in the center of the room. The Arm Chair by the window to be left in the room in it's place by the window. The little four legged table in the corner of the room to be left there. The side board and book case in the arch as they stand. The portrait of Washington—always to hang where it has always—hung over the mantle. The portrait of H.W.L. to remain on the opposite wall. The portrait of father always—to hang where it is now—wad says, unless one of the family wants it. I ADD. The Evangeline leave hanging, the first one made after the poem came out.*

This is only part of the eight pages of instructions that she left. But you can see the bold foresight that she had for the preservation of the home and her stewardship over the contents but, most of all, her respect and love for her family. Anne lived in the home eighty-seven of the ninety years of her life. She was a very strong woman, and after the death of her husband, George Washington Pierce, she returned to the family home. The three years that Anne lived away from the home she referred to as her "little life," and in those three years of marriage, they had no children. The 1930

First of eight pages of instructions left by Anne Longfellow Pierce, circa 1900. *Courtesy of the Collections of Maine Historical Society.*

portrait by Joseph Greenleaf Cole of Anne after her engagement still hangs in the house today. Anne was engaged to George Washington Pierce in 1829. George was from Baldwin, Maine, and studied in her father Stephen's law office. Anne was born on March 3, 1810, one of eight children. Anne wrote of her childhood, "Books and satchels were the ornaments of the parlor table in the evening, and silence the motto, till the lessons were learned—then fun and games were not wanting, and when they grew too fast…for the parlor, the old kitchen rang with our shouts and glee!"

Today, in the kitchen of the house, there is a rocking horse with which the children played. A newspaper article in the files of the Maine Historical

Longfellow children's rocking horse. *Courtesy of the Collections of Maine Historical Society.*

Society mentions Anne's brother Alexander as the person who gave the rocking horse to the Farley family for their children to play with. Alexander said that the horse had served as the rocking horse of his father's family, Henry Wadsworth Longfellow and the other Longfellow children.

Samuel Longfellow, the youngest of the eight Longfellow children, wrote in the biography *Life of Henry Wadsworth Longfellow*:

> *His father could tell him of the theatre in Boston; but the drama seldom came to Portland. The circus and the menagerie were not frequent visitants. Eagerly attended, they were, of course, imitated at home. Feats of grand and lofty tumbling and horsemanship were exhibited for sisters' benefit, the steed being a large wooden rocking horse which stood in the back porch; but family annals record that once vaulting with too great vehemence over the horse's head, he brought the horse over with him, breaking his neck,—fortunately the horse's, not his own.*

The horse was later donated to the Maine Historical Society.

Aunt Lucia was Zipah's sister, and she lived in the house with the family and helped raise the eight Longfellow children. After the death of her parents, Anne lived in the home with Aunt Lucia as a co-owner. Anne became sole owner of the home after the death of Aunt Lucia. She lived to see the changes made in what was the small city of her birth; she watched it grow

Anne Longfellow Pierce, Portland, circa 1890. *Courtesy of the Collections of Maine Historical Society.*

only to watch it burn during the fire of 1866. After the fire, Anne wrote to her sister Mary Greenleaf, "We are all well, unharmed after a most terrific conflagration which sweep through our city last night—beginning near the Sugar House soon after 4 P.M. and burning with tremendous furor till 4 this A.M. and still burning in the corner part of the city. The wind was very high. You have no idea what it is."

After Anne's death, the home became a museum, and a library was later built on the grounds of the home, per Anne's request.

The Children's Gate was designed by Anne's nephew Alexander Wadsworth Longfellow Jr. and is located between the house and the library.

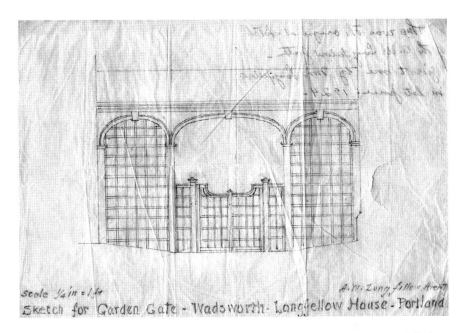

Garden gate sketch, Portland, 1924, by Alexander W. Longfellow Jr. *Courtesy of the Collections of Longfellow Garden Club at Maine Historical Society.*

The Children's Gate, Longfellow Gardens, Portland, circa 1930. *Courtesy of the Collections of Longfellow Garden Club at Maine Historical Society.*

Wadsworth-Longfellow House. *Courtesy of the Collections of Maine Historical Society.*

Entering through the Children's Gate, one finds the Longfellow Gardens, beautiful grounds full of flowers, shrubs and trees maintained by the Longfellow Garden Club. This organization has been in existence since 1924, a group of volunteers that come every year to plant, weed, water and do whatever else is required to keep this beautiful area pristine. Over the years since 1901, the house has been entertaining the public from all over the world, as well as school groups from the state of Maine and beyond. It could never been done without the volunteer docents and paid guides who conduct these tours.

THE LONGFELLOW HOUSE

A Tour Guide's Reflections

By Judie Percival

Let's begin at the very beginning! A very strong-minded nine-year-old was a student at the Longfellow School in Portland, Maine. In the classroom hung large portraits of Henry Wadsworth Longfellow and George Washington, and her class was concentrating on the poetry of Henry Wadsworth Longfellow. She already had memorized to recite "The Psalm of Life" and "My Lost Youth." As her tenth birthday was soon to approach, she had already decided what she most desired: a trip to her favorite poet's boyhood home, the Longfellow House, also in Portland. She received her wish. Yes, I was the little girl!

My name is Judie, and I have been a guide at this historic home for fifteen years—fifty-five years later, returning to Portland retired! In 1999, I was hired by the Maine Historical Society to once again be at my favorite historic site and be a tour guide. I shall endeavor to give my thoughts and reflections on being a tour guide for "the Poet's" Home. It is more than just an honor and a privilege; it's a responsibility to take historic facts and give them life. Each guide is given a booklet that covers complete descriptions of each of the eight rooms and their contents.

Many personal stories are available because the Longfellows were avid letter writers. If you were to go to Harvard's Houghton Library in Cambridge, Massachusetts, there are over eighty boxes of the letters from the Longfellow family. The guides are lucky to have real facts and not fiction designed to impress visitors. Guiding is taking control of your tour. Make a special occasion for all. I still remember—it is still the same, each and every time I enter through the majestic front door, a feeling of "I'M HOME!" In 1999, my first tour, I tried to give the visitor that magical feeling I first felt when, at ten years old, I became enchanted with the simple elegance of years long gone.

Anne Longfellow Pierce, Henry's sister, bequeathed the house to the Maine Historical Society, and her presence is so much there even today. The young Longfellow ladies of the day would study with a private teacher the special courses so designed, including manners, music, sewing and writing. Whereas the young men were subjected to the higher studies of the day, including mathematics; however, Anne was allowed the opportunity to study mathematics and managed a good grade, for which her brother Henry expressed great pride in her accomplishment. These math skills would serve Anne well throughout her many years of keeping control of cost and still providing necessary improvements to the "Old Original" and running a house on a budget. I spell Anne with an *e*, something she herself changed at some point in time. It was not uncommon for young ladies with an English background to do the same. I'm sure I never heard that as a student in Portland, but I, too, changed from Judy to Judie at some point in my youth! Anne's adult role at the Longfellow house modeled her mother, Zilpah, who was a wise parental figure, focusing on absolute manners and politeness and yet extremely understanding and aware of the different needs of her children, reading to them and directing them into adulthood with a gentle firmness.

Here's one more guiding story never put to pen, and this, too, is absolutely true as witnessed by me. It was a Monday afternoon in 2001, and we were very busy at the Longfellow house. Many people were buying tickets. The tours were selling out fast that afternoon. It would have been my fourth and final tour of the day. It already was overbooked, but by only a few, so we would accommodate everyone. As I watched each and every one, I assembled them to go directly to the house, without enough time for the one-on-one conversing. We proceeded to the house. Everyone was happily chatting as we entered the front door, which gives such a nice first impression entering the boyhood home of the poet. We went directly to the best parlor. Everyone was trying to get to their best vantage point when two visitors, completely not aware of anyone else, pushed to be directly in front of me. One never smiled and the other would half smile, but their eyes never left me. Everyone else responded to comments and the family stories. The same positioning occurred in all eight rooms. If for some reason the two visitors were not in the front, they would immediately get to that wanted place. I thought maybe they didn't want to be identified. They never spoke or asked a question.

It was a happy, fun group, and the tour was going very well—questions were asked, and answers were given. I most always end my tours in the front upstairs guest bedchamber. The room was where I would make reference to Henry's passing at the age of seventy-five, and I quote a line from "The Psalm of Life," the first poem of the poet's I had memorized. I made mention that the portion I was about to read was Queen Victoria's favorite poem. "Lives of great men all remind us that we can make our lives sublime and, departing, leave behind us footprints on the sands of time." The same individuals were near me as we started all exiting the front door. I thanked each and every person as they made their exit. The two males left without a word, but as the last few people were exiting, suddenly the more pleasant male returned, stepped in front of an exiting guest and grabbed my hand with both his hands; he shook my hand, half smiled and left! He returned not one more time but a total of three times to acknowledge me. The last two handshakes were normal.

I shall never forget. I couldn't forget him or his friend with the dead eyes, especially having spent one hour in their presence. That was Monday, September 10, 2001, at about three o'clock. On Tuesday, September 11, 2001, at 9:00 a.m., I watched the actual attack of 9/11 on *Good Morning America*. First Tower One and then a small speck heading to the second tower; it was a second plane. I was due to work by 10:00 a.m. and took my small TV into the Maine Historical Society so we could keep up with the happenings. Our visitors gathered around the TV; many were traveling and hadn't heard the news. Then came the announcement that two terrorists had departed the Portland Jetport for Boston at 6:00 a.m., and there at a security checkpoint was a close-up of the two males I had given a tour on Monday. The man with the dead eyes had a name, Atta, and his companion with the half smile, Alomari, who shook my hand three times.

In closing, I highly recommend being a tour guide. The adventure of telling a historic story is a journey into the history of a family, their traditions and principals, taking a journey into the past with an interpretive eye to the future and the fun of a new audience each tour. You never know who might be on a tour—a king, a movie director, an actor, a writer, an editor or another ten-year-old loving the Longfellow house as much as I do. That child may come back many years later to guide yet another child.

Over the years, many souvenirs of the Longfellow house were made and sold. Some of them are quite collectable; the images here are of just a few.

Miniature Longfellow-Wadsworth House pitcher, circa 1910. *Courtesy of the Collections of Maine Historical Society.*

Souvenir plaque of the Wadsworth-Longfellow House, Portland. *Courtesy of the Collections of Maine Historical Society.*

Right: Wadsworth-Longfellow House souvenir vase, circa 1925. *Courtesy of the Collections of Maine Historical Society.*

Below: A Tichnor Brothers postcard of the Wadsworth-Longfellow House in Portland, circa 1928. *Courtesy of the Collections of Boston Public Library.*

BIBLIOGRAPHY

Butler, Joyce. "The Life and Times of Anne Longfellow Pierce." N.p., 2000.

Butler, Joyce, Richard D'Abate and Laura Fecych Sprague. *Henry Wadsworth Longfellow and His Portland Home*. Portland: Maine Historical Society, 2004.

Elwell, Edward H. *Portland and Vicinity*. Portland, ME: Loring, Short & Harmon and W.S. Jones, 1876.

Goold, Nathan. *Longfellow's Old Home: Its History and Its Occupants*. Portland: Maine Historical Society, 1905.

Henry Wadsworth Longfellow. Maine Historical Society, 2005–2012. http://www.hwlongfellow.org.

Hilen, Andrew, ed. *The Letters of Henry Wadsworth Longfellow*. Vol. 1, *1814–1836*, and vol. 2, *1837–1843*. Cambridge, MA: Belknap Press of Harvard University Press, 1966.

Hughes, Libby, and Marian R. Carlson. *American Genius: Henry Wadsworth Longfellow*. Cambridge, MA: Schoolmaster Press, 2006.

Kanes, Candance. "Smallpox in Portland." Maine Historical Society article, 2013.

Levinsky, M. Allan. *The Night the Sky Turned Red: The Story of the Great Portland Maine Fire of July 4, 1866, as Told by Those Who Lived Through It*. Carlisle, MA: Commonwealth Editions, 2014.

———. *A Short History of Portland*. Carlisle, MA: Commonwealth Editions, 2007.

Longfellow, Henry Wadsworth. *Hyperion*. N.p.: Wildside Press, 2007.

———. *Longfellow Poems and Other Writings*. Edited by J.D. McClatchy. New York: Library of America, 2000.

————. *Outre-Mer*. N.p.: Wildside Press, 2007.

Maine Historical Society. "Home: The Longfellow House & the Emergence of Portland." Exhibit, John Mayer, curator, 2014.

Maine Memory Network. Maine Historical Society, 2000–2015. https://www.mainememory.net.

Moulton, John K. *The Portland Observatory: The Building, the Builder, the Maritime Scene*. N.p.: self-published,1996.

Price, H.H., and Gerald Talbot. *Maine's Visible Black History*. Thomaston, ME: Tilbury House Publishers, 2006.

Strum, Harvey. "Smuggling in Maine During the Embargo and the War of 1812." *Colby Quarterly* 19, no. 2 (1983). http://digitalcommons.colby.edu/cgi/viewcontent.cgi?article=2511&context=cq.

Thompson, Lawrance. *Young Longfellow*. New York: Macmilan Company, 1938.

Willis, William. *The History of Portland*. N.p.: Macmillan Company, 1865.

INDEX

M

Maine Charitable Mechanic
    Association 35
Maine Historical Society 48, 127, 133,
    135
Munjoy Hill 19, 27, 59

O

Old Jerusalem 59
Outre-Mer 103, 104, 105, 115

P

Paul, Jean 121
Pierce, George Washington 71, 98,
    103, 111, 127
poetry 22, 43, 54, 55, 57, 68, 69, 73,
    76, 88, 96, 100, 125, 133
Portland 19, 27, 31, 34, 36, 37, 39, 43,
    49, 55, 59, 63, 64, 66, 71, 76,
    81, 85, 89, 90, 94, 96, 99, 113,
    116, 117, 119, 133, 135
Portland Academy 33, 44, 98
Portland Head Light 96
Portland Observatory 19, 59
Potter, Mary 98, 99

R

Round Hill School 106

S

smallpox 59

W

Wadsworth, Peleg 43, 85
War of 1812 29

ABOUT THE AUTHORS

J OHN BABIN is the visitor services manager at the Maine Historical Society. John is responsible for overseeing the paid guides and volunteer docents who give tours in the Wadsworth-Longfellow House, on the Longfellow Trail and the Historic Walking Tours of Portland. John is also the person who coordinates all the K–16 school groups for museum education. John was formerly a docent and site coordinator for the Wadsworth-Longfellow House and is currently serving as a docent at the Victoria Mansion. John holds a real estate broker's license from the State of Maine and is a trained specialist in historic homes and architecture.

A LLAN LEVINSKY, a Portland native, has had three books published: *At Home with the General: A Visit to the Joshua Chamberlain Museum*, *A Short History of Portland* and *The Night the Sky Turned Red: The Story of the Great Portland Maine Fire of July 4, 1866, as Told by Those Who Lived Through It*.

He has had many articles published in newspapers and magazines and has worked in both radio and television. He is now retired after working seventeen years at the Maine Historical Society.

Visit us at
www.historypress.net
....
This title is also available as an e-book